Compassionate Confrontation

A Christian Response to Post-Christian America

Jim Evans

About the Cover

The symbol of the fish bones is a reminder that no matter
how bad the situation may appear, God is able to use even
dry bones to accomplish His purposes.
Perhaps the Lord is speaking to the church today as He did
to Israel when they said,
"Our bones are dried, and our hope is lost."
(Ezekiel 37:11)
But God said,
"Behold, I will cause breath to enter you that you may
come to life. And I will put sinews on you, make flesh grow
back on you, cover you with skin, and put breath in you
that you may come alive;
And you will know that I am the LORD."
Ezekiel 37:4-6

Dedication

This book is dedicated to all the men and women who have
suffered for their faith and found God to be trustworthy
and His grace to be sufficient.

Table of Contents

—ɷ—

Acknowledgements

—⟋w⟍—

The first Person I would like to acknowledge is the Lord Jesus Christ without whom I would still be in a blinded, lost condition that would make this or any other good work impossible.

I also would like to acknowledge my wife, Joan, who has served with me since 1976 and my children who lived and suffered through the circumstances that came as a result of their dad wrestling with the issues that are at the heart of this writing. Without their willingness to stay with me and their faith in God's sovereignty in our circumstances, even when it meant dad going to jail, this book would never have been written.

My thanks to the authors who have shaped my life and my thinking with their writings. Many of them have been quoted in this work and are found as recommended reading at its end.

There are also many men who have mentored me over the years. Pastor Walter Venman, my lifelong pastor, baptized me, oversaw my ordination to ministry, and has been on the other end of my phone over the years as I found myself in situations that required spiritual counsel and prayer. Pastor Bob Roberts challenged me with his deep spiritual life and encouraged me to pursue what I believed I had found as Truth in the Scriptures. He not only showed me how to live but ultimately showed me how to face death as a Christian. Pastor Earl Osborn ignited a passion in me as my professor at Lancaster Bible College and has continued to fan that flame with his mentoring and support throughout the years.

One man whom I never had the privilege of meeting in person but who has had a profound impact on my life and thinking is Dr. Francis Schaeffer. I have read practically everything he has written and while researching this work I have found many of the thoughts I assumed to be original with me are actually sourced in his writings.

There is nothing new under the sun and there is nothing truly original with this author. I have attempted to give credit wherever I am aware of a source outside of myself. In reality even my own thinking can be credited to the influence of my fellow pilgrims on this earthly journey and my heavenly Companion and Counselor, the Holy Spirit, who was given to the Church for the duration of God's plan for mankind on planet Earth.

Preface

—∿∿—

This book is being written to encourage Christians to re-evaluate their response to the present American culture. It is not intended to be negative but rather to be realistic. It comes as a result of thirty years of attempting to be an influence in the world around me and wrestling with the concept of compassionate confrontation.

In the beginning of the book I define the present culture. It is imperative that we understand the reality in which we live. We often avoid confrontation and deny the godless direction that is becoming more and more evident in America, our churches, our families, and our personal lives as we are hoodwinked by the daily influence of a biased media, celebrity soap boxes, and financial influences. As accommodation and tolerance become the demands of our day, we are like the frog that is boiled to death because the heat of the water is increased at a rate that is barely detectible.

In the third chapter I have taken a biblical look at the issue of civil disobedience. Voltaire makes an interesting observation when he says, "It is dangerous to be right in matters on which the established authorities are wrong." Is it possible to be disobedient without being disrespectful? What happens when a Christian finds himself at odds with the law when he is practicing obedience to God?

Chapters four through seven lay down four cornerstones of our response to a godless culture which I summarize as compassionate confrontation. Some will view this type of response as radical but most will agree that this is what a normal Christian response should look like. Search the Scriptures when the subject matter makes you feel uncomfortable. The book is intended to be more than just another book with another interesting viewpoint. Its purpose is to change lives for the glory of God.

Many times the true enemy is within. Our flesh wrestles against the Spirit. (Galatians 5:17) Martin Luther understood this when he said, "I am more afraid of my own heart than of the pope and all his cardinals. I have within me the great pope, Self." May the reader first examine Self before judging others.

The final thing I would have you understand before you begin is that I am still struggling to consistently live all that I propose within these pages. These principles and precepts were learned through years of mistakes and victories. They are intended to be practical rather than another addition to the theoretical theology of a disengaged American Christianity.

POST-CHRISTIAN AMERICA

"Woe to those who call evil good, and good evil.
Who substitute darkness for light and light
for darkness.
Who substitute bitter for sweet, and sweet for bitter!
Woe to those who are wise in their own eyes,
and clever in their own sight!"

Isaiah 5:20-21

CHAPTER ONE

Post-Christian America

—∽∿∿—

A Reality Check in Buffalo

Saturday, April 29, 1989 was a cool spring morning as many pastors and church members gathered at 6:00am to once again go to 260 Elmwood Street in Buffalo, New York. Together they would reach out to young women who were scheduled to have their unborn children killed and draw public attention to one of the five abortion clinics that operated in the Buffalo area.

The scene was typical of other such Saturdays. A gathering of pastors stood nearby praying. A group of about fifty people were sitting in front of the entrance to the abortion clinic and were singing and praying. Several Christian women were walking up and down the sidewalks looking for those who had an appointment at the abortion clinic that morning. They were there to ask women to reconsider their decision to abort their child and to encourage them to see a doctor who would assist them through their difficult pregnancy.

Standing in the parking lot near the police chief, I was on the scene to maintain a peaceful Christian atmosphere among those gathered. Outside the yellow ribbon of the police barrier the milling groups of hostile pro-abortion protestors were shouting to the police, "Do your job, arrest them."

It was a typical morning, and we knew that several babies would be saved and young mothers would receive help and factual information. The subject of abortion in Buffalo would once again make the evening news. It was a scene mixed with songs, flashing police lights, media crews and violent chants from the supporters of abortion.

Meanwhile, one by one those who sat quietly in front of the door of the abortion clinic were being arrested and taken away in police cruisers. They left the scene knowing they had done all they could as Christians to prevent another murder.

All seemed to be going fine until I heard a voice from behind me say, "I want this one!" Read an eye-witness account of what took place that morning:

> At 7:35am I saw at least four Buffalo police drag Rev. Jim Evans approximately 50 yards to a car and open both back doors. Then I saw two officers go around to our side of the car and clearly punch Rev. Jim at least four to five times. (One I recognized as Officer G— from previous marches.) I then shouted for them to stop. Officer G— told me to come in the parking lot to the car and he'd give me some. They then got Rev. Jim in, but his head was clearly still outside when one of the officers slammed the door on Jim's head. They left in car #843. (D. Dissette, personal interview, April 29, 1989)

The following Monday morning I sat across the desk from the police chief in his office at police headquarters. He and I were meeting together to evaluate what took place the previous Saturday. The atmosphere was different than it had been on previous occasions when we met. Neither of us expected to be discussing a police brutality situation.

From the very beginning I recognized that there was going to be a tension between the law which protected abortion and the Christians who wanted to prevent it. Over seventy pastors and many church members had decided that silence was an inappropriate response to child-killing in our community.

The chief and I understood that the issue would put the police and the pro-life Christian community on different sides of the struggle. The chief was bound by duty to uphold a law that protected child-killing, and we were bound by duty to obey the Scriptures that demanded that we "deliver those who are being taken away to death." Proverbs 24:11,12

That the struggle would include the beating of a local pastor by a police officer while the crowd outside the yellow ribbon of the police action cheered him on was unexpected. Suddenly we were engaged in a cultural struggle that was far bigger than either of us had imagined.

With other incidents of police brutality in his file, Officer G—, who attacked me, was relieved of duty. The immediate problems were settled, but the upcoming months would bring a federal investigation upon the police department spear-headed by the abortionists and a sympathetic congressman. In order to intimidate the Christian community, Pastor Ted Cadwallader and I would receive a sixty day sentence for trespassing on the property of an abortion clinic.

How could a God-fearing police chief come under federal investigation for his balanced handling of pro-life Christians? What is wrong in America when two law abiding pastors find themselves cast into prison for trying to save the lives of unborn children and assist women in crisis? That Monday morning the chief and I spoke about the issues at hand, but the uncertainty of the future had now exposed itself, and neither one of us was comfortable with what we saw.

America is Changing

It is now 2007. The Federal Access to Clinic Entrances Act, which makes it a federal felony to get in the way of someone headed to an abortion clinic, has slowed down Christian participation in rescue missions. Homosexuals have made great strides in legalizing their immoral behavior. Children in public schools who consider sodomy to be sin are subject to sensitivity training. The ACLU is challenging the government's right to restrict pornographic material on the internet. Violence continues to increase, teen suicide is at an all time high, and the public schools still maintain atheistic evolution as their exclusive doctrine of human origins. Underneath all this is an increasing anti-Christian bias within the judiciary.

Christmas of 2005 was rife with controversy as people attempted to celebrate the season with traditional nativity scenes and Christmas carols. For many generations Americans have sung carols and set up manger scenes at Christmas. However, this year would be different. It seems that these traditional Christmas symbols are somehow offensive to certain individuals and radically out of line with the culture of the new America. Towns, malls and even some stores, threatened by potential lawsuits and unwanted controversy, decided to change their verbiage to "Happy Holidays" and to refrain from placing nativity scenes in their Christmas displays.

Several years ago I noticed that our local bank had a Christmas tree, Santa Claus, and a menorah decorating the bank but no nativity scene. I asked the bank manager if she would accept and display a small nativity scene if our ministry donated one to the bank. Uncertain about the bank policy she made several phone calls to various people and was told by a corporate attorney that she could display it, but if there were any customer complaints it would have to be removed.

We purchased a small nativity scene and she happily placed it in the middle of the decorations that adorned the teller windows. There were also several angel figurines provided by some bank tellers to accompany it. For three years this nativity scene had occupied the same central place. Last year I went to the bank during the Christmas season and noticed that the nativity scene was missing from all the decorations. I inquired concerning its whereabouts and was told they must have forgotten to get it out. The next day it was placed at the far right-hand side of the teller windows. It was obviously a cautiously concealed corner and certainly no longer central to the theme. I know the bank manager loves the nativity scene and there was even a sense of victory among the tellers as I courteously suggested that Christ's birth was what Christmas is all about and that the nativity scene, should be brought out of storage.

What had intimidated my friends at the bank to fear this Christmas symbol? Even the greeting "Merry Christmas" was to be avoided in public if one was to fall in line with the new politically correct society and avoid being considered radical.

Lines are Being Drawn

Consider this letter to the editor written by eleven-year-old Jasmine Botta in the December 23, 2005 Letters to the Editor section of the Town-Crier, a Wellington, Florida newspaper. She was challenging the current direction our nation appears to be headed. She was also thankful that the Wellington town council had recanted of its previous ruling and was now allowing the nativity scene to be displayed on village property among the various other holiday and religious symbols. Here are her words (edited for length purposes):

What's going to happen to us if we keep on ignoring God? The same thing that happened to all the other countries that have tried to ignore God. God punished them.

What happened to Adam and Eve when the devil tricked them into eating the forbidden fruit by saying they would be equal to God if they ate the fruit? . . .

God will punish us like all the other countries that have ignored God. Nobody can live without our Lord. God will get very mad if we take "one nation under God" out of the Pledge of Allegiance. If we don't change our ways soon, God will punish us, too.

In Wellington, we could not put up a nativity because the government of Wellington said religion and government couldn't coexist. Fortunately, the government of Wellington later reconsidered and placed a simple nativity next to the menorah for all to enjoy. I think that was a wise move, because it's one little step closer to salvation.

In the old America Jasmine would have been seen as a Christian girl who had a good handle on what it means to be a good citizen. After all, she is following in the great footsteps of Thomas Jefferson, the author of the so-called "wall of separation" who said, "Indeed I tremble for my country when I reflect that God is just, and His justice cannot sleep forever." But we no longer live in the old America. The next week two loyal citizens of the new America stepped up to rebuke and set Jasmine straight. Rev. Marjorie Weiss, a local pastor wrote:

Eleven-year-old Jasmine Botta's recent letter to the editor about our country ignoring God and facing punishment made me so very sad that I feel compelled to write.

Is God a punishing God? The theology of many Christians would say no. . . .

Saddest of all is that far too many Christians pass on these warped ideas of a punishing God. You have heard it: God punished the Pacific nations with the tsunami as most were Muslim and not Christian; God punished New Orleans for its decadent lifestyle; God punishes gays with AIDS. Such thinking makes Christians look like the very evil that we purport to be against. (emphasis mine)

The next concerned citizen to attempt to set Jasmine straight was Andrew Rosen who wrote:

I am writing this short note in response to the letter by Jasmine Botta, age 11, in your issue of Dec. 23. I understand that she is only 11 and has not had the proper history classes to fully understand what she is saying, but unfortunately, what came out in her letter was that unless people believe in her God, they are doomed (i.e., the Aztecs). . . .

Jasmine, also please read the history of people who have believed in the same God as you. Look at Europe in the Middle Ages when religion ruled. *The wars and injustices caused by these people in the name of the God you believe in were terrible.* Learning came to a virtual standstill if it went against the church's viewpoint. . . .

I hope that after reading this note, Jasmine, you will be more tolerant of people's beliefs and understand that whether people believe in God or not, in your God or not, we all need to work together to make things in the world better. Intolerance only leads to harm, violence and danger. One does not need to go back to the Middle Ages to see this, it is currently happening all over the world. (emphasis mine)

So much for Jamine being a good Christian citizen. According to today's standards, she is an intolerant, uneducated person and an example of the reason for many of the wars and injustices in the world. Even a religious leader sees her as the product of warped ideas.

What has Happened?

Did we lose a war? Has some foreign power taken over our nation? We still vote. We still have a semblance of freedom. We are still looked upon as the template of a free democracy. Why then is the core of our traditional lifestyle and Christian heritage under attack from within? We have misunderstood what makes our nation great. The greatness of our nation is based on more than the right to vote, or unrestrained freedom, or even democracy but rather it is based on the foundation of God's law and His blessing.

Our country has been attacked from within. While the social mores and core values of our culture were being rewritten in the name of pluralism and inclusiveness, the Christian faith was being pushed into a church building and out of America's public life. There is a desire on the part of many to remove all evidences of the Christian faith that proclaims a living, loving, holy God who will judge all people. Since it is impossible to totally remove Christianity from our culture it has been surrounded by a "great wall of separation" and considered irrelevant to real life issues. The very teachings that were central to the founding of our nation have been set aside.

Although I disagree with Jon Meacham's attempt at putting words in the minds of our founding Fathers as he does in his book, <u>American Gospel: God, the Founding Fathers, and the Making of a Nation</u>, he does emphasize the important role that religion plays in shaping the culture of our nation. He notes that America is, in its political makeup, neither totally secular nor religious but rather a place where the influence of both brings about the American success story.

The removal of the influence of God's Word in our land is like removing light from a dark room. It has very significant implications. Not darkness, but a lessening of light is what is destroying our land. The fallen culture is by nature dark. This is the dark/light imagery of the Gospel throughout the New Testament. Consider the following as a small sample:

All things came into being by Him, and apart from Him nothing came into being that has come into being. In Him was life, and the life was the light of men. And the light shines in the darkness, and the darkness did not comprehend it. John 1:3-5

And this is the judgment, that the light is come into the world, and men loved the darkness rather than the light; for their deeds were evil. For everyone who does evil hates the light, and does not come to the light, lest his deeds should be exposed. But he who practices the truth comes to the light, that his deeds may be manifested as having been wrought in God. John 3:18-21

And do not participate in the unfruitful deeds of darkness, but instead even expose them; for it is disgraceful even to speak of the things which are done by them in secret. But all things become visible when they are exposed by the light, for everything that becomes visible is light. Ephesians 5:11-14

Back in the days when I thought spooky stuff was cool, my friends and I would drive to a vine covered stone wall near where we lived. The wall was about eight feet high and served as a retaining wall for a hill on which a barn stood.

Used as a dog kennel, the barn attracted hoards of rats. These rats lived in the stone wall and would climb on the vines at night. We would pull our car up to the hillside and shine our lights on the wall. The wall was alive with rats enjoying their romp on the vines! But as soon as the light hit the wall they would retreat into the shelter of the rocks. When we turned the lights off the rats would soon come out of hiding and dominate the wall again.

In the daylight a couple could stroll, hand-in-hand, along the wall without fear or anxiety but when the light was taken away the wall became a very different and spooky place. Were the rats there in the daytime? Sure they were, but they avoided the vulnerability of being exposed by light and stayed out of sight.

The same is true of our culture. If we remove the light of the influence of the Word of God from our culture it will cease being the blessed and enjoyable country it was in the daylight. It will give safe haven to the wicked and promote evil. In a very systematic way the influence of God's Word is being removed from our land.

Exclusion from the Public Square

What was once smug exclusion has become an assumed legal injunction of restraint that prevents public school teachers from merely referencing the Bible, school children from praying, nativities from being placed on public property at Christmas time, and a host of other anti-religion or more precisely, anti-Christian public policies. The new politically correct landscape is full of rushing rivers of intolerance that are slowly wearing away at the Christian foundations of this nation. As one looks around, the words of Dorothy when she considered the oddities of Oz become quite appropriate, "Toto, I've a feeling we're not in Kansas anymore."

Violent crime is on the increase, divorce is commonplace, sodomy is now considered a lifestyle instead of a sin, pornography is accepted entertainment, traditional marriage is under attack, and atheism, especially in the academic world, is in vogue.

If Ben Franklin was still our emissary in France he would no longer be able to describe America as he did in a pamphlet entitled *"Information to Those Who Would Remove to America."* In his description of our land he wrote, "Bad examples to youth are more rare in America, which must be a comfortable consideration to parents. To this may be truly added, that serious religion, under its various denominations, is not only tolerated but respected and practiced. Atheism is unknown there; infidelity rare and secret; so that persons may live to a great age in that country without having their piety shocked by meeting with either an Atheist or an Infidel." Note that freedom of religion included the free practice of all Christian sects or denominations. This was the strong opinion of the great patriot Patrick Henry. He wanted no mistake to be made concerning what guides this nation through the dense and dangerous forest of history. He declared, "It cannot be emphasized too strongly or too often that this great nation was founded, not by religionists, but by Christians; not on religions, but on the gospel of Jesus Christ!"

Exclusion from Science

Science also guards its turf from Christian participation in research and discovery. The evolutionary theory, the genesis or theory of origins of both secular and religious Humanism and of communist atheism, has been established as the only theory permitted in the scientific arena. Although evolution is just as much a religious theory as the theory of creation or more recently the theory of intelligent design, it is held up as being more scientific.

Alan D. Gishlick, critic of challenges to evolution says, "Evolution is the unifying paradigm, the organizing prin-ciple of biology. A paradigm functions as the glue that holds an entire field together, connecting disparate sub-fields and relating them to one another." In other words, if evolution isn't right then a lot of other conclusions of modern science based on this assumption may be suspect also.

Evolution is the system that fits the first tenet of Humanism which says that there is no super-natural. Everything happened without a god or intelligent being. Somehow, somewhere, energy and matter collided and began a process of upward evolution that became all that we see today. Evolution is the lid that keeps God in the box of religion and out of the real world and especially science.

In a PBS series, *The Question of God*, Armand Nicholi brings a panel together to consider the worldviews of Sigmund Freud and C.S. Lewis. His premise was this: "Whether we realize it or not, all of us possess a worldview. We make one of two basic assumptions. We view the universe as an accident, or we assume intelligence beyond the universe who gives the universe order, and for some of us, meaning to life."

Michael Shermer, one of the seven panelists, explains his worldview as: "Naturalism is my philosophy. That all phenomenon have natural explanations. There is no super-natural, there's just the natural and stuff we can't yet explain. " If one were to permit that evolutionary assumption to be removed, science would come face-to-face with the true and living creator God. The safely contrived higher power in counseling circles and intelligent agent in renegade scientific groups would be specifically defined.

Does a person like Michael Shermer have an objective scientific basis for his worldview? Here is his explanation in his own words: "My philosophy is that all phenomenons have natural explanations. There is no supernatural, there's just the natural and stuff we can't yet explain. That's basically my position. Socially, when I moved from theism to atheism and science as a worldview, I guess, to be honest, I just liked the people in science, and the scientists, and their books, and just the lifestyle, and the way of living. I liked that better than the religious books, the religious people I was hanging out with — just socially. It just felt more comfortable for me." (from: PBS Program – The Question of God, Program 1, Conversation 1, "A Transcendent Experience")

It is very uncomfortable for science to entertain the thought that there is a supernatural and that there may be a God who exists outside the system of natural cause and effect. Christianity and its scientific theories are randomly excluded based on the unfounded assumptions of the scientific elite.

Exclusion from Education

With evolution as its paradigm and the basis of its worldview, our public school systems have completely reversed the historical values and ethics once held as indispensable to our nation's future. For more than two generations the children of America have been taught that they evolved from some primitive form, morals are personal, and there are no absolutes. The New America teaches that religious people are intolerant, foolish, and prudish. They claim that prayer, the Bible, and Jesus Christ are irrelevant to the real world, and people are free to experiment and do whatever makes them feel good. Planned Parenthood has found a breeding ground in our schools for its sexual revolution and has held children hostage from their parents as they provide provocative and perverse sexual misinformation. Condoms and abortions are given to minor children without parental knowledge or consent!

Publications in our schools encourage sexual experimentation which includes homosexuality, multiple partner experiences, and all forms of perverse sexual behavior. All this is said to be normal, and any prohibitions are the misguided, prudish opinions of religious bigots or at best, out of touch old people. Our tax dollars have funded these teachings, our laws now protect the behavior they produce, and our health-care costs support the results of their perversions. Sodomy, bisexuality, abortion, pornography, and all sorts of perversions are accepted as a part of normal living, and those who oppose such behavior are classified as intolerant.

Moreover, these perversions are increasingly protected by a tyrannical judicial system that has found a way to nullify the will of the people and ignore the guidance of the constitution and the corresponding historical documents that interpret its meaning. The great reformer Martin Luther once accurately prophesied, "I am much afraid that schools will prove to be great gates of Hell unless they diligently labor in explaining the Holy Scriptures, engraving them in the hearts of youth. I advise no one to place his child where the Scriptures do not reign paramount. Every institution in which men are not increasingly occupied with the Word of God must become corrupt."

The use of the public school to attack the church is a planned strategy of the humanist movement in America. Read what Paul Blanshard wrote in an article in *The Humanist* titled, Three Cheers for Our Secular State:

I think that the most important factor moving us toward a secular society has been the educational factor. Our schools may not teach Johnny to read properly, but the fact that Johnny is in school until he is sixteen tends to lead toward the elimination of religious superstition. The average American child now acquires a high school education, and this militates against Adam and Eve and all other myths of alleged history. . . When I was one of the editors of *The Nation* in the twenties, I wrote an editorial explaining that golf and intelligence were the two primary reasons that men did not attend church. Perhaps I would now say golf and a high school diploma.

All this is a far cry from the founding mission statement of Harvard University which demonstrates the original goal of education in America. "Let every student be plainly instructed, and earnestly pressed, to consider well the main end of his life and studies is to know God and Jesus Christ which is eternal life, John 17:3, and therefore to lay Christ in the bottom, as the only foundation of all sound knowledge and learning."

The New America

Is it any wonder why our country is in the process of totally eradicating Christianity from its culture? What was once an editorial opinion written by a radical humanist in the twenties has now become popular consensus.

True, we have not been invaded or defeated in the military sense. However, the government and principles that guided this nation for its first 230 years have been successfully dismantled or held hostage by the new pioneers of Humanism being sent out of our secular colleges and universities to change the world. Abraham Lincoln warned us that the teachings in the school of one generation would be the doctrines of government in the next. Daniel Webster adds, "If there is anything in my thoughts or style to commend, the credit is due to my parents for instilling in me an early love of the Scriptures. If we abide by the principles taught in the Bible, our country will go on prospering and to prosper; but if we and our posterity neglect its instructions and authority, no man can tell how sudden a catastrophe may overwhelm us and bury all our glory in profound obscurity." Just how close are we to that catastrophe today?

In the aftermath of the recent massacre at Virginia Tech many questions are being asked. There has been a rise in mass killing in America in the past two decades. James Alan Fox, professor of criminal justice at Northeastern University, ponders these things as he writes:

So what has changed? For one thing, the United States has become much more dog-eat-dog, more competitive in recent years. We admire those who achieve at any cost, and it seems that we have less compassion for those who fail. (Just look at how eager we are to vote people off the island or to reject them in singing competitions.) This certainly increases frustration on the part of losers.

Then there's the eclipse of traditional community: higher rates of divorce, the decline of church-going and the fact that more people live in urban areas, where they may not even know their neighbors. If mass murderers are isolated people who lack support, these trends only exacerbate the situation.

Like Mr. Fox we can all ask and answer the question, "What has changed?" We all recognize that we live in a new America. The question is: "Who is responsible for this change and how could it have gone so wrong?"

The emissary of this new America is the media. It has promoted the perverse values of this new world. It has mocked and belittled the conquered masses that were too busy with their lives to even notice this subtle invasion. This new America advocates freedom for all, but censorship only for the Christian. It boasts of a "do as you wish" agenda.

It appears that unless America changes its direction our freedom will be as short lived as that one which the Israelites experienced when godly leadership gave way to corruption in their government. The book of Judges continually reminds us that when governmental righteousness is not ruling, man will inevitably partake of evil. The phrase "and Israel <u>again</u> did evil" is the social result of "every man did what was right in his own eyes." Time and again we learn that what is right in our eyes is often evil in the eyes of God. The collapse of nations throughout history can be traced to their moral decline and corruption.

Do any of the following slogans sound familiar? "We can have morality without religion." "Whatever is legal is moral." "Morality cannot be legislated." "Pornography is a harmless adult pleasure." "You shouldn't mix religion and politics." "Religion is a private matter and has no place in government or politics." "What happens behind closed doors is no one's business." "You can always turn the TV off."

These are the slogans of the new America. They are used to justify sinful behavior and to imply that what is on TV and what is declared legal behind closed doors will not have a negative impact on our culture, our country, and our future. These values are totally foreign to the old America. The devastating effect of secular and religious humanists on our culture is as real and oppressive as a military conquest by a foreign government. Listen to George Washington: "It is impossible to rightly govern the world without God and the Bible." Or consider Thomas Jefferson: "God who gave us life gave us liberty. Can the liberties of a nation be secure when we have removed a conviction that these liberties are the gift of God?"

Sadly, the Bible is a censored book in this new America, but be reminded what President Woodrow Wilson had to say, "The Bible is the one supreme source of revelation of the meaning of life, the nature of God, and spiritual nature and need of men. It is the only guide of life which really leads the spirit in the way of peace and salvation." John Quincy Adams said, "The first and almost the only book deserving of universal attention is the Bible." Noah Webster tells us that, "The moral principles and precepts contained in the Scriptures ought to form the basis of all our civil constitutions and laws. All the miseries and evils which men suffer from vice, crime, ambition, injustice, oppression, slavery and war, proceed from their despising or neglecting the precepts contained in the Bible." The United States Supreme Court decision of 1892 in the Church of the Holy Trinity v. United States opinion declared that:

> Our laws and our institutions must necessarily be based upon and embody the teachings of the Redeemer of mankind. It is impossible that it should be otherwise; and in this sense and to this extent our civilization and our institutions are emphatically Christian. . . This is a religious people. This is historically true. From the discovery of this continent to the present hour, there is a single voice making this affirmation . . . we find everywhere a clear recognition of the same truth. . . These, and many other matters which might be noticed, add a volume of unofficial declarations to the mass of organic utterances that this is a Christian nation.

Rev. Robert Schenck tells of his conversation with a school administrator in a recently freed Russian Republic. With tears in her eyes she implored him, "Please, go back to your country and tell the American people not to forget God. We are like those lost in the forest without a compass. For seventy-four long and terrible years, the government would not allow us to hear about God. Now our young people do not know what is right or wrong, good or bad, truth or a lie. Please, tell your people they do not want to be where we have been."

Our Challenge

We must stop imagining that everything is alright and realize that Christians and the true church no longer enjoy the privilege of living in a culture that is supportive of Christianity. Today we live in a nation where we can expect controversy, confrontation, and intimidation. We will experience more legal threats and actions attempting to make us recant of our confidence in one true and living God. This is the God who created all that exists, who rules in the affairs of mankind, and who will one day return in judgment to set all things straight. We must accept the title of radical if being radical means living for Christ — even if it is contrary to popular opinion. Voltaire was right when he said, "It is dangerous to be right in matters on which the established authorities are wrong."

When I use the term post-Christian America I do not mean that people no longer profess to be Christian or no longer attend church. Most people will say they are Christian and many are regularly attending church. By post-Christian I mean that most Americans no longer base their lifestyle and philosophies on Judeo-Christian doctrines.

It is obvious that the courts and legislatures along with the academic elitists have removed reference to or dependence upon the Word of God in their rulings, laws, or teachings, but it is sad to realize that the established church has done virtually the same thing in practice.

Several years ago I was involved in a lengthy and heated debate on the nature of the child in the womb and what position a particular local Bible-believing church should take on the abortion issue. The Scriptures appeared to carry no more weight than personal experience, opinion, and pseudo-scientific theories. Many who professed to be Christians gave verbal homage to the Bible and then added a transitional "but" followed by the reason we could not base our church policy on such a narrow and outdated viewpoint.

A culture is Christian when most of its members rely on the ethics and morals revealed in the Bible when dealing with the issues of life. It is a non-Christian (or in our case, a post-Christian) culture when the majority of its members no longer live by the lifestyle and morals given in the Bible, even if they do profess to be Christians and do attend church.

Francis Schaeffer warned of this day in many of his writings. Near the close of his book, <u>The Great Evangelical Disaster</u> he wrote these words: "We cannot think that all of this is unrelated to us. It will all come crashing down unless you and I and each one of us who loves the Lord and his church are willing to act."

There is a need for the voice of God in the land of the godless. It should not be a voice of judgment but a voice of warning. Not a voice of condemnation but a voice of compassionate confrontation, wishing for none to perish but for all to come to repentance. We must proclaim the Word of the living God to a dying people. Will America perish for want of a prophet? Will the prophet stand a chance in the public square? Can America bear to hear the Word of God from the people of God?

The enemy is truly plotting against Christ and His followers. In a recent article from USA Today the question is posed: "Is God dead in Europe? (And what might that mean for America?)" The author, James Gannon, goes on to tell of Prague now being classified as Europe's new capital for the pornographic film industry, and that only 19% of the people of the once religious country of the Czech Republic now believe in God. Nate and Leah Seppanen Anderson wrote in the *Prague Post*: "Common wisdom has it that alcoholics out-number practicing Christians and that more Czechs believe in UFOs than believe in God – and common wisdom may be correct."

George Weigel, a Catholic columnist and U.S. biographer of Pope John Paul II says, "A fierce controversy over any mention of Europe's Christian heritage erupted in 2004 when officials were drafting a constitution for the European Union. Many argued that any mention of the continent's religious past or contributions of Christian culture in a preface citing the sources of Europe's distinct civilization would be exclusionary and offensive to non-Christians." Former

French president Valery Giscard d'Estaing, who presided over the process, summed up the dominate view: "Europeans live in a purely secular political system where religion does not play an important role." Could it be that the Berlin wall came down because the other side had won the Cold War of ideology?

The New America is dominated by a culture that has rejected all that it was founded upon. It has become a strange place to those of us who were raised up in the Christian culture that dominated the America of the past. The new inhabitants of our land are now ready to silence the Truth and its messengers. For the first time in the history of America the Bible is a censored book, and Christianity is an oppressed religion.

RESPONDING TO A HOSTILE ENVIRONMENT

"No totalitarian authority nor authoritarian state can tolerate those who have an absolute by which to judge that state and its actions. The Christians had that absolute in God's revelation. Because the Christians had an absolute, universal standard by which to judge not only personal morals but the state, they were counted as enemies of totalitarian Rome and were thrown to the beasts."

Francis A. Schaeffer, <u>How Shall We Then Live</u>?

CHAPTER TWO

Responding to a Hostile Environment

—ɱ—

Fight or Flight

How should the Christian respond when the public practice of his faith is opposed and in many cases declared illegal? What happens when the police show up to arrest your pastor? Jesus was in a garden with some of his disciples when the police showed up to take him to jail for publicly preaching against the wicked culture of the day and for judging the behavior of men by the Word of the Lord. Peter, a loyal follower of Jesus, stepped forward and cut an ear off the arresting officer. Jesus told him to put down the sword. He then restored the arresting officer's ear. Christ did not come to battle for a temporary earthly kingdom but rather to lay hold of an eternal, spiritual kingdom. His battle was against principalities and powers in heavenly places, not against flesh and blood.

The historic account of this event tells us that all the disciples scattered. After all, this was the Roman government that was now taking action against them. It seems that we as humans either take up the sword or surrender; take back the culture or hide out in the church. Peter followed Jesus at a safe distance, probably still hoping to do something to rescue Him, which sounds a lot like the posture the American Christian has taken. Eventually, as he tried to hide out in the community, he was recognized as one of Jesus' followers. It is interesting that after his second denial of being one of "those who were with Jesus," he was pointed out as a Jesus follower because he talked differently than everyone else. Matthew tells us that he "began to curse and swear" in order to fit in. Luke tells us this is when Jesus looked at him, and he remembered the Lord had previously told him he would deny Him. He wept bitterly. His denial and attempt at self preservation seemed to work until he "remembered the Word of the Lord," at which time he wept bitterly at the recognition of his betrayal of the One he had earlier declared to be the Son of the Living God. (Matthew 26:34-75)

Our own tendency toward self preservation often runs parallel to Peter's as we participate in comfort-zone Churchianity that attempts to blend into the hostile environment around us. Romans chapter 12 encourages us to stop being conformed or schemed into the world around us but rather to be transformed by the renewing of our minds. At some point we must realize that the Lord is watching us. Then we may finally remember the Word of the Lord and come face-to-face with the depth of our compromise. But even if we are willing to confess that we are living in a compromised way, what are the alternatives?

How should the Church respond to the growing hostility toward the Word of God and those who believe it? Many American Christians believe that God has called us to silent piety. By this I mean that what the world does is none of our business, and they know where we stand. You have heard, "As long as they don't force me to have an abortion, then it is none of my business." Or possibly you have heard, "I can always put my children in Christian school instead of public school." All around us the culture is demanding that we as Christians condone sinful lifestyles by our silence.

We tell ourselves, "Only the Gospel can change America, we should not get caught up in issues." Being a former drug addict, I completely agree that the Gospel of Jesus Christ is man's only hope. But what is the Gospel? Is it that Jesus can make you happier? Or Jesus can make you more prosperous? Or maybe Jesus can raise your social standing? Tell that to a man rolling in money, women, and vice. He couldn't be happier as far as he is concerned. He is relatively prosperous. After all, he throws his keys to a valet to park his new BMW at one of the best restaurants in town where he rubs shoulders with some of society's finest. Most lost people actually believe they have a better life than most Christians. They are convinced that they enjoy life more.

Sure they have divorces, but don't Christians? Sure they get into financial trouble, but don't Christians? Sure they may cheat a little, lie a little, get drunk a little, and do some things they aren't proud of, but don't Christians also have these problems? "So," they ponder, "if we are all about the same, why should I join up with a bunch of people that add restrictions on life, guilt, and required church attendance to my already hectic life?"

The True Gospel

The Gospel is being sold as something that gives you a better life when we should be warning that the Gospel is the only source of life. The Scriptures clearly teach: "He who has the Son has the life; he who does not have the Son of God does not have the life." (1 John 5:12) At the heart of the Gospel is the acknowledgment and recognition of the penalty of sin, which is death. The lost are literally the walking dead. The sentence of death and hell are upon them because by nature, we are all the children of wrath. (Ephesians 2:3-9)

The lost are like a happy, pipe smoking fisherman who has terminal lung cancer and doesn't want to believe it. He continues happily on his way, ignoring all the warnings and concern of the medical community. His friends are afraid to confront him about his plight because he seems so happy, and they know he hates doctors and hospitals with a passion.

Shouldn't we be warning our neighbors of the consequences of sin? Isn't vigilance our responsibility as Christians? Consider what the Lord said to one of the religious leaders of Israel:

Son of man, I have appointed you a watchman to the house of Israel; whenever you hear a word from My mouth, warn them from Me. "When I say to the wicked, 'You shall surely die'; and you do not warn him or speak out to warn the wicked from his wicked way that he may live, that wicked man shall die in his iniquity, but his blood I will require at your hand. Yet if you have warned the wicked, and he does not turn from his wickedness or from his wicked way, he shall die in his iniquity; but you have delivered yourself. Ezekiel 3:17-19

Now, along the same lines, look at what He says to us as Christians living in the present time:

For you were formerly darkness, but now you are light in the Lord; walk as children of light (for the fruit of the light consists in all goodness and righteousness and truth), trying to learn what is pleasing to the Lord. And do not participate in the unfruitful deeds of darkness, but instead even expose them; for it is disgraceful even to speak of the things which are done by them in secret. Ephesians 5:8-13

We are told that we are no longer in darkness, therefore we are responsible to walk in goodness, righteousness, and truth. And while we are struggling to learn what is pleasing to the Lord, we are to avoid the lifestyle of the world, and instead we are to expose it. We are to shed some light on the issues of life. Could this mean a letter to the editor, a press conference, or a talk with the neighbor?

We preach about sin in our churches and give solid nods and quiet "Amens" to the reminder of the condemnation it brings. Then a large majority of the church membership goes out to work and play; where they make jokes about those same sins, and in some cases they even practice them. What is the problem? Nobody wakes up in the morning and looks forward to being a hypocrite. Allow me to suggest two reasons for this situation. First, some of the people who say "amen" on Sunday are lost and are unable to live any differently on Monday. Secondly, there are the real Christians who, like Lot of old, are vexed in their righteous souls on Monday. The problem is, we all hate to be hated. It is a natural impulse or desire to be accepted. Sometimes it behooves us to remember how the world treated some of our early brothers and sisters:

> They were stoned, they were sawn in two, they were tempted, they were put to death with the sword; they went about in sheepskins, in goatskins, being destitute, afflicted, ill-treated (<u>men of whom the world was not worthy</u>), wandering in deserts and mountains and caves and holes in the ground. And all these, having gained approval through their faith, did not receive what was promised, because God had provided something better for us, so that apart from us they should not be made perfect. Hebrews 11:37-40 *Emphasis mine.*

The Gospel in Our Culture

You may claim that these were people that lived back in a less civilized time when the culture was against them. We live in a Christian nation, and that will not happen here. Let's move forward then to 1999 in Littleton, Colorado, the heartland of America.

Rachel Scott was a fun loving Christian girl who once stuffed twenty-four marshmallows into her mouth to win a "Chubby Bunny" contest. Her teachers said she obviously loved life. She was a girl whose smile lighted the room she entered and whose loyalty to Christ made many of her friends uncomfortable. One of her journal entries included these words:

> If I have to sacrifice everything . . . I will. I will take it. If my friends have to become my enemies for me to be with my best friend, Jesus, then that's fine with me. I always knew that part of being a Christian is having enemies . . . but I never thought that my friends were going to be those enemies.

In another entry she asked God, "Why can't I be used by You?" Little did she realize that she was going to be used in a way that would go far beyond what she could ever imagine. She was destined to be more than a Sunday school teacher, more than a Bible study leader, more than an evangelist. This young Columbine High School student from Littleton, Colorado was about to become a martyr for her faith.

A gun wielding fellow classmate was taking a survey one morning at the school. He was asking his fellow classmates, "Do you believe in God?" Rachel's friend Cassie was heard responding "yes" to the question. Speculation would assume that Rachel did the same. In the midst of these heavenly confessions of faith, all hell broke loose on earth as gunshots echoed through the hallways of Columbine High School.

Simultaneously in heaven, Jesus, who was seated at the right-hand of God, rose to His feet to welcome these young Christians home as He has done many times for martyrs down through the ages. The impact of their youthful martyrdom touched the lives of thousands of people around the world. Though they were taken from the earth their testimony will continue to call people to unconditional surrender to the Lord for years to come.

Wouldn't it be great if the heartfelt words Rachel wrote in her private journal were etched in each of our hearts and became the guiding principle of our lives? Were Rachel and her friends unbalanced radicals? Did they bring the condemnation of this boy upon themselves by being so outspoken and uncompromising in their public Christian testimony? Not at all! Their walk was the same as God-fearing Christians down through the centuries. Rachel's testimony was one of joy, love, life, and a true concern for others. She believed God and attempted to warn others.

The haters of God would naturally target her and people like her because she spoke and lived God's Word and caused them to face the reality of the terminal disease of sin they carried about in their bodies and souls. But the irony of this scenario, which is filled with anger and death, is that it happened in the context of the practice of unconditional love. For you see, it is true love that warns, real love that reaches out, sincere love that helps, and unselfish love that gets involved. Remember the admonishment of the Scriptures:

> For this is the message which you have heard from the beginning, that we should love one another; not as Cain, who was of the evil one, and slew his brother. And for what reason did he slay him? Because his deeds were evil, and his brother's were righteous. Do not marvel, brethren, if the world hates you. We know

that we have passed out of death into life, because we love the brethren. 1 John 3:11-14

Rachel and her friends lived by the truth of God's Word. Why is it then that the American Christian knows little of this type of suffering? Is our land so Christian and our culture so godly that it is a friend of God and the citizens of His Kingdom?

The fact is that this world hates the Truth and hates to be reminded that judgment day is coming. Our culture is unbothered by people having a religion, but they are bothered when they hear about right and wrong, or that God judges sin, or that there is a hell to be avoided and a heaven to be attained.

A Deal Has Been Made

Back in the late sixties there was a rather controversial debate held between a Christian leader and an attorney for the ACLU over religious freedom in America. The ACLU was claiming that Americans had religious freedom. The Christian leader was saying that restricting the Bible and prayer in schools while imposing the mandatory teaching of evolution (which contradicted the religious beliefs of the majority of Americans) was evidence that we do not have religious freedom. The attorney said that people have the freedom to worship whatever they wanted, whenever they wanted but a person's private religion can not be imposed on the public. The attorney's statement expresses how the ACLU looks at religious freedom:

> The American Civil Liberties Union has a long history of working to ensure that religious liberty is protected. From the famous 1920 Scopes trial- in which the ACLU challenged a Tennessee law prohibiting the teaching of evolution in schools

–to the current Ten Commandments case before the Supreme Court, the ACLU remains committed to keeping the government out of the religion business and protecting every American's right to believe as he or she wishes." (American Civil Liberties Union, 2005, p. 1)

Defending the teaching of the theory of evolution while refusing to allow the teaching of creation as an alternative theory is hardly to be considered defending religious freedom and "protecting every American's right to believe as he or she wishes." What if an American wants to believe in creation? Refusing to allow the Ten Commandments to be posted or referred to in schools where all sorts of other cultural norms, mores, and vices are taught is hardly protecting religious rights.

The attorney's summation of his position is a commentary on the quiet religious treaty of our times. He said that religious freedom is a personal freedom that has no place in the public arena. Everyone is free to worship whatever and whenever he or she wants but not necessarily wherever. The ACLU's interpretation of religious liberty is freedom <u>from</u> religion not freedom of religion.

Religion, by its very design, requires public access and public debate. After all, religion is an attempt to know who man is, why he is here, what he should do, and where he is headed. Christianity is failing in the public debate because it fails to enter the debate. The public square is filled with the state religion of humanism that says man evolved from a lower form of life, he is here due to chance, and he will no longer exist when his physical body ceases functioning. The result is that promiscuity, abortion, sodomy, and other doctrines of humanism are accepted while marriages crumble, teens commit suicide, and all sorts of new psychological terms are given to people who are depressed, angry, and disillusioned.

In other words the deal was this: "We won't bother you as long as you keep your religion on your church property and out of politics, the school, and the public square. You have freedom of religion but you can't force your religion on others." It is in this context that some westerners declared that the Soviet Union had religious freedom because they saw churches where various religions were functioning. However, that freedom ended at the door of the church building. The USSR was an atheistic secular society that guarded its people from the myths and warped ideas of Christianity.

Religious Freedom

This sounds similar to the religious freedom found in Rome in the first century. Rome was a pantheistic society. Many legal religious practices were performed within its borders. The society tolerated these practices as long as Caesar was acknowledged as supreme, and there was no civil unrest caused by conflicting religions or extremists.

But Christianity challenged the existing religious cults because it was not a system of theories but a system of truth and absolutes. It did not speculate about things spiritual but had hard answers to spiritual questions. Christianity's proponents were not merely religious people, they were Christian people, many of whom witnessed the resurrection of Jesus the Christ. Their faith was characterized by confidence, joy, peace, and courage.

In a society where educational and philosophical heritage established the pecking order of social influence, these Christians stood out as a strange sort. In a world of debate and speculation, they seemed to have found objective reality. Note this small snapshot given to us from history:

Now as they observed the confidence of Peter and John, and understood that they were uneducated and untrained men, they were marveling, and began to recognize them as having been with Jesus. . . . "But in order that it may not spread any further among the people, let us (*the religious leaders*) warn them to speak no more to any man in this name." And when they had summoned them, they commanded them not to speak or teach at all in the name of Jesus. But Peter and John answered and said to them, "Whether it is right in the sight of God to give heed to you rather than to God, you be the judge; for we cannot stop speaking what we have seen and heard." Acts 4:13-19 (*italics mine*)

The world has always had an ACLU or similar watchdogs that try to cut a deal with God's people. In the preceding passage, the religious attorneys said you can no longer preach in name of Jesus. It says they threatened them. Here was their response: "Let's see, obey God or obey you guys; what do you think we ought to do?" They continued preaching the Gospel and confronting cultural sins in the name of Jesus.

Personal Agendas

In 1985 I became deeply grieved over the public silence of most of the evangelical church concerning abortion. Desiring to make a difference, I put together a project that would help churches respond to abortion in a way that exposed it for what it really was. The project was called Moratorium on Murder. The acronym "M.O.M." signified the cry of the unborn. It was designed to set aside one day to interrupt business-as-usual at abortion clinics throughout the land by picketing, praying, and counseling young mothers.

Since my desire was that the moratorium have a national impact, I drove to Washington DC to enlist the aid of some national pro-life leaders. I knew that there were national events held in larger cities, but this project could reach into the small towns and involve all sorts of churches. To my surprise, I was greeted as an outsider and found the heads of various organizations to be very territorial.

This would be another lesson in how the enemy has divided and diluted the Christian voice in America. One leader of a large pro-life group told me that they hesitate to use the word "murder" concerning abortion because of a lawsuit filed in Alaska. I asked him if he believed that abortion was murder. He said that technically it was a misuse of the word because abortion was legal, and murder was a legal term that meant the illegal taking of life.

We often promote our personal agendas and find it difficult to unite with others who are engaged in the same battle. We guard our verbiage because of the threat of lawsuits and hedge our words because we may lose the support of a political party. In reality we compromise God's truth for fear of sounding intolerant or being snubbed by our friends or family. This attitude has become so customary and accepted that we are unaware of what we are doing.

If the truth of the Christian faith is in fact Truth, then it must be practiced both in teaching and practical action. Truth demands confrontation since it stands in antithesis to the teaching and practice of error. It must be a loving confrontation, but there must be confrontation nonetheless. The twentieth century church accommodated cultural myths and concealed real truth because of the threats and difficulties that come when the two cultures collide. The twenty-first century church appears to be holding the same course.

Limiting the Influence of God's Word

You might say, "How did we conceal real truth?" First of all, we concealed it by limiting the sphere of its exposure. Also, we retreated back inside the four walls of our church compounds. At best, programs were designed to encourage us to go out at least one night a week and try to win someone to Jesus. Consequently, we failed to enter the cultural debate on some of the most important issues of human life. Sure, we did not condone the blatant practice of sodomy within the church but we acted as though it would not matter if the culture became convinced that it was an alternative lifestyle or a gene-based reality rather than a sinful practice. And now child killing (abortion) continues as though it was a medical procedure that corrects a sad but personal crisis. The centers of debate, i.e. newspapers, talk shows, magazines, and other outlets are virtually devoid of the Christian voice, with the exception of a few national lightning rods that have been deemed as non-representative of true Christianity.

Callum Brown, professor of religious and cultural history at the University of Dundee gets to the root of the demise of the Christian culture in England when he writes, "The culture of Christianity slid without much murmur, without a battle of wills between free-thinkers and churchmen." In the same article he makes reference to the Michael Parkinson televised talk show that hosted England's Tony Blair on March 4, 2006. Blair referred back to his early introduction to politics by saying, "There were people at the university who got me into politics, I kind of got into religion and politics at the same time, in a way." He was then asked if it (religion) still influenced his view of politics and the world. Blair answered, "Well, I think if you have a religious belief it does, but it is probably best not to take it too far." Herein lies the mood of the age in which we live. Religion is fine as long as it accommodates the autonomous freedom that humanism demands. Just how far can one take one's religious beliefs? At what point do we set aside what we believe in order to accommodate what we know to be wrong?

As Jesus approached the Mount of Olives, a multitude of followers began to cry out, "Blessed is the King who comes in the Name of the Lord." This statement was politically incorrect in an empire where Caesar was king. It was troubling to the religious leaders of the day who had a comfortable pact with the Roman government. These religious leaders, either because they feared government retaliation or because they were guarding their religious turf, demanded that Jesus make His disciples be silent. His response was interesting. He said if they become silent the rocks will begin to cry out.

In light of the silence of the church in America, I have been expecting the rocks to cry out for the past twenty years. This may be why an eleven-year-old girl felt it necessary to write a letter to the editor of her local newspaper that challenges our culture with the Truth.

Making the Word of God Irrelevant

Not only do we conceal the truth by limiting the sphere of its exposure, but we also lessen the relevance of its warnings. We adopt the absurd sacred/secular dichotomy that keeps biblical truth out of real life. This may explain why a Christian can "Amen" something on Sunday and contradict it on Monday morning as he or she faces the real world. Nevertheless, Truth is truth. If what we learn on Sunday morning or read in our Bibles during our private Bible study is not Truth on Monday morning, then we are of all men most to be pitied.

When the Corinthian church was being challenged about the reality of the resurrection, the apostle Paul reminded them that without the resurrection they would still be in their sin. The thought that Christians were backing down on one of the core doctrines of their faith caused the apostle to take them to task in his letter:

> If from human motives [*rather than doctrinal Truth*]
> I fought with wild beasts at Ephesus, what does it
> profit me? If the dead are not raised, let us eat and

drink, for tomorrow we die. Do not be deceived: Bad company corrupts good morals. Become sober-minded as you ought, and stop sinning; for some have no knowledge of God. I speak this to your shame. 1 Corinthians 15:32-34

Paul did not mince words. He said they were sinning by compromising this doctrine in public. He reminded them that there were lost people out there who needed to hear the truth about a loving creator God who paid the price for man's sin by dying on the cross and rising again from the dead to forever conquer sin, death, and the grave.

Notice that he pointed to the problem of hanging around the water fountain with people who are intolerant of absolutes. (Do not be deceived: Bad company corrupts good morals.) Corinth was a crossroad mecca of marketing and intellectuals. In order to stay "in" with the crowd, the Corinthian believers were willing to be less than confident in the truth of God's Word. Paul said, "Shame on you."

Os Guinness in his book, Prophetic Untimeliness, suggests that we have become outward directed as a society rather than inward directed. Our grandparents lived as though they had swallowed gyroscopes, but we live as though we have swallowed Gallup polls. Christianity has moved from moral (the practice of virtue because we know it is right) to respectable (the practice of virtue because we are seen). The movement of the past decade has been from respectable to hypocritical (the practice of virtue because we are afraid of being seen as bad).

This was the condition of the religious people of Jesus' day. He called them whitened sepulchers full of dead man's bones. He said they were white-washed on the outside but on the inside they were black with death. They were putting on a front to hide what they really were. Hypocrisy is one step away from outright wickedness which abandons any pretense of virtue of any kind. It claims virtue to be a personal opinion, and anyone who claims otherwise is intolerant and unacceptable.

Backing Away from Confrontation

Besides limiting the scope of God's truth and lessening its relevance to everyday life, we have also concealed the truth by backing away from it when confronted by a hostile world. I have great respect and admiration for William Bennett, former Secretary of Education under President Reagan. While I was running for a seat in the New York State Assembly in 1990, I attended a small reception at a private home in Westchester County, New York. Herb London, the Conservative Party candidate for Governor of New York, had invited me as his guest. Also attending the event were Peggy Noonan and William Bennett. They both earned my admiration as some of the rare people who had been exposed to the toxic elements of the Washington D.C. political scene and maintained their humility, their intelligence, and strangely enough, even their convictions.

Several weeks after meeting Mr. Bennett, I was watching him being drilled on television about the campaign platform of his friend Pat Buchanan. Bennett was asked, "So what do you make of Pat's extreme stand against abortion?" I sat up and waited for a strong endorsement of the platform plank but instead saw Mr. Bennett get a small smile on his face, tilt his head as he nodded, and said, "Oh, that's just Pat." The bullet had been dodged by Mr. Bennett, but I felt like I suffered collateral damage as my heart sank, and I began to realize the power of political intimidation. This is a character flaw that is not limited to William Bennett. It is more common in each of us than we like to think. My mind went back to that small courtyard where the interviewer said to Peter, "Aren't you one of His followers." Jesus was the one tuned into that interview and heard one of his closest followers say, "No, not me. I don't know Him."

We should not be seeking confrontation, but it will seek us because Truth stands eternally in confrontation to error. There is a need for us to understand the biblical principle of compassionate confrontation. This is not confrontation in order to put down, win the debate, or prove oneself right. The goal of compassionate confrontation is to see the Truth liberate someone being held in the bondage of error. We do not have to defend the Truth but rather present it and let it stand on its own. This is the type of confrontation we see in Jesus as He ministered in an upside-down world. We see Paul practice this type of confrontation when he was before judges and rulers.

Bad news is hard to share. People shy away from the topics of reality and absolutes. But if they remain without confrontation, that is, compassionate confrontation with Truth, they will never have the opportunity to experience true freedom. Remember it was Jesus who said the Truth will set you free. We are not called to back away from confrontation but to graciously stand and desire that the Truth will accomplish its work to the glory of God.

Condemnation by Association

Over the past two decades, intimidation by association has been a very effective tool of the secular culture. When courageous Christians become the target of the culture, they are first defamed through the secular news media, and then they are portrayed as examples of intolerant radicals or fanatics. This is done so that others will refuse to stand with them or behave like them. People who supported or identified with the apostle Paul were also confronted with the same strategy. Consider the situation Jason faced for showing hospitality to Paul:

But the Jews, becoming jealous and taking along some wicked men from the market place, formed a mob and set the city in an uproar; and coming upon the house of Jason, they were seeking to bring them (*Paul and his associates*) out to the people. And when they did not find them, they began dragging Jason and some brethren before the city authorities, shouting, "These men who have upset the world have come here also; <u>and Jason has welcomed them, and they all act contrary to the decrees of Caesar, saying that there is another king, Jesus.</u>" And they stirred up the crowd and the city authorities who heard these things. And when they had received a pledge from Jason and the others, they released them. Acts 17:4-9 (*italics and emphasis mine*)

Condemnation by association has been an effective tactic for centuries. Paul was painted as one "who had upset the world," and Jason was accused of welcoming this radical. We must be very careful when we join in with the world when they attack a fellow Christian. Many times we are unaware of the facts, especially if we are dependent on the media or gossip network to provide them.

This is not to say that we must always agree with everything a so-called Christian leader says. Recently, during an ongoing dialog in a local paper concerning whether God will judge the sin of our nation, I was said to be like Pastor X who had a website of hateful rhetoric. I have become accustomed to the reality that when the Truth cannot be denied, people will resort to condemnation by association. I looked up this pastor's website and found the accusation of a hateful spirit to be correct. I responded and said that I disagreed with Pastor X if he is of the mindset that is portrayed on his website.

We stand before God as our Judge and rely on the Scriptures as our Guide. God knows that the life of a disciple is not easy. He knows the true nature of our fallen world and the challenges we must face as His children. As a Father giving a departing encouragement to His children He said:

> Behold, I send you out as sheep in the midst of wolves; therefore be shrewd as serpents, and innocent as doves. But beware of men; for they will deliver you up to the courts, and scourge you in their synagogues; and you shall even be brought before governors and kings <u>for My sake, as a testimony to them and to the Gentiles</u>. Matt 10:16-18 *Emphasis mine.*

One morning in Wichita, Kansas, I found myself in a awkward situation. It was one of those decisive moments that challenges the human spirit and makes you feel like your theology is a tad radical. This was a time when the sacrifices of living for Christ would challenge my comfort zone and personal plans once again.

While I was involved in a political campaign in the 124th Assembly District in upstate New York, I was asked to be the police liaison for what was being billed as a "Summer of Mercy" in Wichita, Kansas. Over a hundred pastors and churches were ready to expose one of the most notorious third-trimester child killers in America. My initial reaction was to stay clear of what was obviously going to become a very controversial event. I was already known as a strongly pro-life candidate, so my participation in opposing late-term abortion would be a non-issue. But if I was arrested in the process, it would surely eliminate any hope of my making a significant impact on the political environment of New York.

Ultimately, I agreed to serve as Police Liaison and meet with the police, political leaders, and the pastors in Wichita to accomplish the project in a way that would be God honoring and effective. The fact that I did not want to be put in a situation whereby I would be arrested was clearly stated.

I flew to Wichita four weeks before the rescues and demonstrations were to begin. Just an hour after I landed, I was stopped by federal agents, and my rental car was searched. There was no justifiable cause to stop me, but I gave no resistance to the unwarranted search which clearly violated my Constitutional rights. They searched the car, found nothing, and let me go on my way. I used the occasion to educate the agents about the details of Dr. Tiller's practice of killing and incinerating late term babies. This type of harassment is becoming more commonplace for those who challenge the morality of the current culture. Instead of seeing situations like this as an attack, we must begin to view these as opportunities to minister to people and "to be a testimony to them and the Gentiles."

My goal was to meet with the police to talk with them about the tactics of non-violent intervention on the behalf of unborn children who were scheduled to be executed and cremated at Dr. George Tiller's "death camp," a.k.a. abortion clinic. We would try to limit collateral problems as much as possible by considering the impact our presence would have on adjoining businesses, traffic movement, and the proximity of playgrounds and schools.

Four weeks later, over seventeen hundred people arrived in Wichita to assist the churches of the city in rescuing children from scheduled execution. They had come to Wichita to expose the practices of George Tiller and to raise awareness of the ongoing slaughter of unborn children in America.

On this particular morning the pro-life rescuers were sitting and singing in front of the gates that led into the compound. Two federal marshals approached me and asked if I knew the whereabouts of Randall Terry, the controversial founder of Operation Rescue. I said that I had seen him at a rally the night before but had no knowledge of his schedule on that day. They said that they wanted him to allow them to escort a young lady into the abortion clinic. I assured them that he was unable to fulfill their request and that we had several medical doctors on hand that would help any girl with free medical treatment.

Obviously frustrated, they handed me an injunction written by a federal judge that prohibited named people from participating in the demonstrations. I had seen the injunction the night before and knew that my name was not on it. I told the marshals that it was improper if not illegal to serve someone with an injunction who was not named on it, but they persisted.

If I permitted this injunction to be used against me and encouraged its use to intimidate non-violent protestors of abortion, it would send a chill over the entire Christian community that had stepped forward to follow the principle found in Proverbs 24:11,12. If I resisted its illegal application, I would be arrested and appear before the federal judge who issued it. My campaign back home weighed heavily on my mind. This decision could cost me all the work and funds that had been expended on the campaign and be a fatal blow to any hope of even a respectable standing on election-day.

As I considered my personal sacrifice, I realized it was really nothing compared to the sacrifice of those who had gone before me. The thought of more bodies being incinerated in the furnace that was only twenty yards behind me within the chained fence surrounding the abortion clinic made my decision simple. I held my hands out as the officers placed handcuffs on my wrists. Moments later Randall Terry and another pro-life leader appeared and were placed under arrest without hesitation.

Soon we were standing before Judge Kelly, the federal judge who had issued the injunction. The judge looked at Randall Terry and said he had seen enough on television to demonstrate that Mr. Terry was in contempt of his court, and he sentenced him to jail until such time as he recanted of his contempt. What he had witnessed on television were news clips of the rally the night before where Mr. Terry called the injunction toilet paper and tore it up. The other pro-life leader was asked if he was of the same opinion concerning the injunction as Mr. Terry, and upon his positive response, he was escorted off to jail also.

The judge looked at me and said, "Mr. Evans, we have a problem with your arrest in that you were not named in the injunction." I assured him that I tried to explain the problem to the arresting officers. Believing that God controls our circumstances, I took the opportunity to address the court. I said, "Your honor, with all due respect, I want you to understand that I disagree with Mr. Terry in regards to this injunction. I believe it to be a federal document that has the force of the federal government behind it. You have every right to issue such injunctions, just as the federal judges of Nazi Germany had the right to issue injunctions against assisting and abetting Jews in their escape from the legally operating death camps. I could not have obeyed those injunctions, and I am not able, as a matter of conscience, to obey this injunction that prohibits me from aiding and rescuing unborn children from the death camp located in Wichita, Kansas."

Did this mean that I was opposing Randall Terry? No, it meant that I believed Randall was wrong in his approach to authority. Tearing up an injunction is good theatrics, but it stands in opposition to the biblical admonishment to respect those in authority. (We will look more deeply into that subject in the next chapter.) It also flew in the face of the examples we have in the Bible of godly people who had to disobey the authorities in order to obey God. The Scriptures stand as the ultimate judge of all our actions and attitudes.

Following this principle causes the world to do battle with the infallible Word of God and removes the tendency toward individual attacks. I believe the judge respected my position even though he recommended I leave town.

Later that day, as I was speaking to a local pastor, about fifty yards from the abortion clinic, two federal marshals stopped and told me they were sent to place me under arrest for violating the injunction. (My name had been hand-written into the injunction earlier that day with no hearing to show cause nor opportunity to present a defense. An injunction restricts normal constitutional rights, and evidence must be presented to justify these restrictions. The target of the injunction must also be given opportunity to defend those rights.) I asked them how I had violated the injunction, but they said they had no details. The judge had ordered them to apprehend me and bring me before his bench. It was late in the day when the marshals tried to contact the judge to get more details, but he was gone for the day. They had no alternative but to take me to the detention center where I would spend the night in jail and appear before the judge in the morning.

The next morning prosecutors brought three trumped up charges against me. The judge recognized they were trying to use his court to fight their battle. He found no grounds for their charges and rebuked the prosecutor because I had to spend a night in jail due to their false charges.

This is the kind of respect even those who appear to be against us will have if we are seen as people of integrity. We were still on the opposite sides of the issue, and I would certainly have to pay the consequences if I violated his injunction, but it was no longer a personal battle but rather a battle of principles and Truth. This is a battle the Christian can not lose because it has been forever won at Calvary.

Avoiding Being Thrown to the Beasts

We can avoid being thrown to the beasts by continuing to abide by a treaty of silence, or we can begin to understand the implications of disobedience to God and unrestrained public sin. Daniel had a problem when he was asked to violate God's dietary instructions for the Jewish people. He respectfully requested a different diet and promised that it would prove to be even more beneficial to the king. Later, an injunction was issued that put Daniel's faith under fire again. In a smoke filled room at the capitol, a little meeting was held. Here is an excerpt from the meeting:

> All the commissioners of the kingdom, the prefects and the satraps, the high officials and the governors have consulted together that the king should establish a statute and enforce an injunction that anyone who makes a petition to any god or man besides you, O king, for thirty days, shall be cast into the lions' den. Daniel 6:7

Daniel had a problem. He was named in the injunction in the phrase "anyone," and he was being prohibited from obeying God by praying to Him and Him alone.

If Daniel were attending a church board meeting about this predicament in today's climate, he would be told, "Look, this is only for 30 days, and it has nothing to do with the Messianic message anyway, so we ought to obey it. God wants us to obey those in authority over us, and maybe we could just have a couple small prayer times in secluded places over the next month. Surely God doesn't want us thrown into the lion's den, and besides that, if we disobey the king he could really make it hard on us. Remember that lesson guide we got from that big conference speaker that said disobeying the law is an example of rebellion and disregard for God-ordained government authority."

Daniel would really be under pressure if he were a Christian today trying to obey God and the civil authorities. The church would be divided on the issue, so he would be in conflict with half the authorities of the church besides disobeying the government. Here was his decision.

Now <u>when Daniel knew that the document was signed</u>, he entered his house (now in his roof chamber he had windows open toward Jerusalem); and he continued kneeling on his knees three times a day, praying and giving thanks before his God, as he had been doing previously. Daniel 6:10 (*emphasis mine*)

Daniel was brought before the king for his violation of the injunction. The king knew Daniel to be a man of character and regretted having to apply the law to him. But he was obligated to his duty, and ordered Daniel thrown to the beasts. All night long neither he nor Daniel got much sleep. The lions, however, must have slept, because they failed to harm Daniel. The next morning the king was actually relieved to find Daniel alive and attributed this miraculous deliverance to Daniel's God. He ordered Daniel's accusers to be fed to the hungry lions. Daniel explains it this way:

My God sent His angel and shut the lions' mouths, and they have not harmed me, inasmuch as I was found innocent before Him; and also toward you, O king, I have committed no crime. Daniel 6:22-23

Our silent piety may temporarily keep us from being thrown to the beasts, but it has also robbed our culture of a desperately needed warning and the good news of redemption. Additionally, it has robbed God of the occasion to glorify His name in our land.

A Stirring is Taking Place

According to recent polls done by George Barna, Christian pollster, there is a stirring taking place within the established church. Many strong Christians are becoming disillusioned with established churches that are failing to engage the culture with practical Christianity.

It seems that we have professionalized the ministry and franchised the church. Pastors seek promotions and high places while churches limp along trying to control their current pastor or look for a new one. It is as though we are marketing hamburgers. Some people prefer McDonalds, some Wendys, some Hardees, and then there are the contemporary sorts that like Lindburgers. Churches compete with other churches for the largest congregation, the most contemporary worship music, or the most famous pastor. The focus is upon the church and its programs. I call this Church-ianity.

When church-ianity gives way to Christianity, we will see a cultural awakening along with the greatest persecution of Christians in this nation since the eighteenth century, when non-licensed Baptist ministers were imprisoned and beaten. We must never forget that <u>all</u> those who want to live godly lives and do more than just attend church will suffer persecution (2 Timothy 3:12). This persecution could range from losing good friends, to imprisonment, or even being martyred.

I have heard it said that Christians who have suffered persecution in America have "brought it on themselves" by breaking the law and refusing to submit to God-ordained authority. Is this true? This topic is becoming more and more important to us as the laws in America become less Bible-based and more humanistic.

Salt in a salt shaker is a potentially active, but dormant compound. When it comes out of the salt shaker and lands on its target, it becomes active and accomplishes what it was designed to do. The same is true of the Christian sitting in the pew of the established church. The inactivated potential residing within the evangelical church could turn the world upside down. This potential includes the moral influence, the gospel outreach, the financial resources, and the godly models that the world so desperately needs and the enemy of God so vehemently wants to keep bottled up.

When the salt leaves the salt shaker, it becomes active and causes a reaction in the element to which it is applied. It is used up in accomplishing its purpose of seasoning and preserving. So, who wants to jump out of a comfortable church compound into enemy territory and risk getting used up or being thrown to the beasts as the world reacts to the presence of Christian Truth? This is the challenge – to return to the only Christianity Peter, John and Paul knew!

American General Billy Mitchell had such a concept in mind when he submitted a proposal during the First World War that envisioned dropping soldiers by parachute behind enemy lines. Since it was assumed that it was inappropriate to force men to jump out of an airplane, and the handful that would be crazy enough to volunteer was too small to make an impact, no action was taken by the American military to further develop the concept of paratroops.

In July 1940, First Lieutenant William T. Ryder, from the 29th Infantry Regiment, volunteered to participate in a trial paratrooper platoon. He was designated the test platoon's leader. Forty-eight enlisted men were selected from a pool of two hundred volunteers. The first jump from an aircraft in flight was made at Lawson Field on August 13, 1940 by members of the test platoon. There was a sense of excitement among the men.

The test platoon held a lottery before the drop to determine who would have the opportunity and privilege to follow Lieutenant Ryder out of the airplane and become the first enlisted man to parachute from a C-33. Private William N. (Red) King placed second in the lottery, but after the lottery winner declined to jump, he was given a place in history. I wonder what the parachutist who won the lottery thought. I have researched this history in many sources and have been unable to find his name. He has been renamed by history as the-lottery-winner-who-would-not-jump. This man gave up perhaps the one chance he had in his life to go down in history and to be what he professed to be.

The first sentence of the Parachutist Creed speaks of the heart of those willing to step forward. It reads, "I volunteered as a parachutist, fully realizing the hazard of my chosen service and by my thoughts and actions will always uphold the prestige, honor and high esprit-de-corps of parachute troops." Notice that an airborne soldier is a volunteer soldier. He is aware of the hazard of his decision, and he has committed both his thoughts and his actions to the responsibility of living up to the high standards of his calling. The airborne soldier becomes what we must be – active agents within the very holdings of the enemy.

A Challenge is Being Offered

God seems be to be forming up a new airborne division in His Church. These are people who have caught a vision of a spiritual opportunity that takes the battle deep into enemy territory in order to free prisoners of war and hasten the victory. They are willing to jump out of comfort-zone Church-ianity to apply the salt of God's Truth to a godless culture.

These are regular people who know in their heart-of-hearts that sitting in a pew on Sunday and having private devotions while living in compromise and intimidation is the antithesis to what we find in the Bible and is unpleasing to the Lord.

Placing your name in such a lottery is easy, but when God calls your number, will you go, or will history rename you the-called-one-of-God-who-would-not-go?

Radical Christians are an unusual group of people. You can usually spot them in a crowd, because there is something about the peace and confidence they have and the focus they have on people. They seem to love the people whom others avoid. They serve in areas others won't consider and can be seen standing tall and calm when others want to run and hide.

I served twenty-seven months in Phu Bia, Vietnam with the 101st Airborne Division and have an unusual bond with frontline Vietnam vets. Likewise, in thirty-three years on the frontlines of God's ministry, I have experienced the esprit-de-corps between authentic Christians who have surrendered their lives to God's purposes.

I invite you to join the ranks of radical Christians who are unwilling to be bribed with the comforts of this world or intimidated by its threats. Radical Christians genuinely love all people, honor civil government, and sincerely obey God in all things no matter what the cost.

So, when people look at you and ask why you are so radical, maybe you can tell them:

"I volunteered as a servant of the Lord, fully realizing the hazard of my chosen service. By my thoughts and actions I will always uphold the prestige, honor and high esprit-de-corps of a citizen of God's Kingdom."

RESPONDING TO THOSE IN AUTHORITY

And when they had brought them,
they stood them before the Council.
And the high priest questioned them, saying,
"We gave you strict orders not to continue
teaching in this name, and behold,
you have filled Jerusalem with your teaching,
and intend to bring this man's blood upon us."
But Peter and the apostles answered and said,
"We must obey God rather than men."

Acts 5:27-29

CHAPTER THREE

Responding to Those in Authority

—⚂—

What is civil disobedience?

Civil disobedience is a symbolic or intentional violation of a law deemed unjust, rather than a rejection of the system as a whole. Generally, civil disobedience follows the assumed futility of using other avenues and legal means of addressing a perceived social problem. By submitting to punishment, those who disobey an unjust law hope to set a moral example that will provoke the majority or the government into effecting political, social, or economic change.

The philosophical roots of civil disobedience lie deep in Western thought. America's founders often appealed to systems of natural law that take precedence over the laws created by communities or states (positive law). Some more recent examples of civil disobedience include Sir Desmond TuTu, a South African Anglican cleric, who encouraged peaceful protest against apartheid and later won the Nobel Peace Prize for his actions. Martin Luther King, Jr. advocated non-violent civil disobedience to expose the injustice of segregation. Today we find that a small handful of Christians believe that in order to obey the laws of God they must violate the unjust laws of man that protect the killing of unborn children.

The Pittsburgh Nightmare

March 11, 1989. It had been a cold night in Pittsburgh as temperatures dropped to 33 degrees. Early the next morning a group of pro-life demonstrators gathered at the Women's Health Services abortion clinic to non-violently prevent the killing of unwanted children. The temperature would rise to a pleasant 60 degrees, very comfortable for March in Pittsburgh. Many pro-abortion demonstrators had come to counter-demonstrate and to encourage the rapid arrest and removal of those using peaceful civil disobedience to disrupt the scheduled activities of the abortion clinic and to draw attention to the issue of abortion. The pro-life demonstrators were motivated by the conclusion each had reached after being challenged with the question, "If abortion is murder, why don't we act like it is murder?"

Considering themselves to be good citizens bravely trying to stop the killing of unwanted children, each one had agreed to peacefully sit in front of the clinic door. Each had been taught that respect for the police and the authorities was expected, and each had signed a card saying they would listen to the organized leadership and abide by the peaceful nature of the demonstration.

Of the one hundred and twenty people arrested that day, sixty of them were women who ranged in age from late teens to early seventies. Little could they know that, behind the tinted windows of police buses and in the dark shadows of the correctional facilities, a series of abuses and violence awaited them. A governmental fury was unleashed against these pro-life women that would later become known as the "Pittsburgh Nightmare." Each woman knew that she was risking arrest when she placed herself in front of the abortion clinic door to prevent it from opening. They were prepared to pay the price of non-violent, peaceful, civil disobedience in order to save the lives of children and expose the atrocities of abortion, but no one was prepared for the treatment they received at the hands of the police that day.

The shouting of pro-abortion demonstrators and the vulgar, vicious insults were now considered normal and expected at such events. The incidental push, jab, or spit from angry onlookers were commonplace also. But the frustration of the police officers seemed excessive for a demonstration of this sort. Beyond that, what was totally unexpected were the actions of the arresting officers and later the correctional personnel after the arrests had been made.

Women testified of dozens of lewd comments and a few threats of rape from the police officers who incarcerated them. Young women, with their breasts exposed, were dragged through the prison in sight of male prisoners. They were subjected to strip searches while male guards looked on. One young woman with asthma had cigarette smoke deliberately blown in her face until she suffered a severe asthmatic attack and required emergency medical care. An elderly grandmother was threatened with rape and told she would be put in a cell with male convicts.

Rosanna Weissert, a lawyer who once served as Deputy Attorney General for the Commonwealth of Pennsylvania became involved in the case. "We tried to file complaints with the local magistrate," Weissert recalled. But at that first level the pro-lifers were told, "since you can't identify the guards, we can't take the charges." The women reported that, in violation of standard policy, the guards had worn neither badges nor name tags on the day of the arrests.

Next, Weissert sought for a probe by county officials, but their response was merely a paperwork investigation, she says. "They took complaints from the women, which they reduced to writing. The warden said they had no case and closed the file." Several months later the women received copies of their complaints, stamped "Not Approved."

The plaintiffs missed the deadline for filing the appropriate certification for a class-action lawsuit. When the judge assigned to the case ruled that the plaintiffs had thereby lost their right to class-action treatment, the number of plaintiffs suddenly dropped from sixty to five. Three of the five women still involved in the lawsuit chose to accept an out-of-court settlement rather than pressing the case to trial. Attorney Weissert explains that these women were offered a $4,000 payment—which, in effect, appeared to constitute an admission that the women had been wronged. On the other hand, the women were told if they continued to push for their claims and finally lost the case they might be required to pay the defendants' legal fees.

Were these women wrong in breaking a trespass law in order to prevent an abortion? Were the police justified in their actions that day? Strangely enough, many Christians would say these women got what they deserved. Is there a time when civil disobedience is a proper and possibly spiritual behavior for the Christian?

The Controversy

To say the least, there is a controversy in Christianity concerning civil disobedience. We can line up notable Christian leaders on both sides of this important issue. During the height of abortion protests and in particular the peaceful blocking of abortion clinic entrances that took place in the late 1980's, the Christian community was very divided in their opinions concerning what was taking place.

At that time my wife and I were serving as missionaries with a church planting mission. I was the Associate Director of the mission and was establishing a new church near the headquarters office in up-state New York. I was also among the seventy local pastors who led their congregations to address the problem of five abortion clinics in the area that killed hundreds of unwanted children each month.

After meeting with the leadership of the small church that I was helping to form, it was confirmed that they were supportive of our participation in the anti-abortion activities which included the peaceful blocking of clinic entrances. I also met with the board of the mission, and they expressed no real problem with my involvement as a local pastor of a local church. My wife and I met with the Director of the mission in our living room to be sure he understood the controversy around the subject and that it could lead to arrest. He and his wife seemed to have no problems with our involvement.

The issue was still very hypothetical, and there was no desire on the part of the mission board to get into a passionate debate with their associate director over something that, at the present, seemed to be causing no problem. After all, seventy evangelical pastors in the area were involved, and they were seeing many people in their churches becoming spiritually challenged and committed.

The day came when another pastor and myself were singled out as leaders of the demonstrations. Pastor Ted Cadwallader and I were arrested for trespassing just as others that day, but the judge placed a $100 bail on us. Bail was not being used for its legal purpose of holding over accused defendants who might not appear for future court proceedings, but instead it was being used as a deterrent or intimidation. We decided to go to jail rather than pay unwarranted bail. The publicity of our imprisonment also raised the rumblings of controversy. Upon hearing of my arrest, the director of the mission rushed home from meetings in Florida. The controversy had now come to the door of the mission.

I wrote a letter to the Board of Directors to explain the biblical examples of God's people sometimes ending up in jail, and to confirm that, from my perspective, my imprisonment was not a problem but rather an opportunity. Knowing that the imprisonment had put a lot of pressure on the organization, I also offered my resignation. My resignation was accepted, and I was told to vacate my office over the weekend, "before any media shows up." There was a fear that some of the mission's contributors would be opposed to what I was doing and would stop giving.

I was also told to move my family from the staff housing before my fellow missionaries came for a spring retreat that was being held at headquarters. My supporting churches were contacted, and our family lost 95% of our ministry support over the next two months.

When I tried to discuss the situation with people, there was an underlying assumption that Christians should never break the law, and that issues like abortion were non-issues unless Christians were forced to have abortions. I would hear the names of notable Christian leaders who stood against civil disobedience.

There were also many notable Christian leaders who were supportive of the rescue movement, made significant contributions, and publicly commended the efforts of participants. The issue became "whose camp are you in" rather than "what is the right thing to do." There is a tendency for all of us to huddle with supporters rather than do the hard work of digging in the Scriptures for the proper answer.

Critical Thinkers Needed

There is a great need for critical thinkers in this age. I was an adjunct professor at a large Christian liberal arts university where I taught a course on inquiry and analysis. This course sharpens the student's skill level in finding and analyzing data. Finding data is no problem today. Analyzing data is very difficult however. The student must learn the discipline of being a critical thinker. He must learn to become objective and honest about the data or issue he is researching. Most of us follow popular opinion, peer opinion, or personal opinion without researching the data that is necessary to have a legitimate opinion.

We profess to be people that live by the commands, limits, and examples put forth in the Bible. This is one of the core values of the evangelical Christian community. It separates the evangelical from the religious humanist who adapts God's Word to contemporary circumstances rather than judging contemporary circumstances by God's Word. We laugh at some of the absurdities of politically correct (PC) jargon but fail to realize that we have fallen prey to theologically correct (TC) jargon. The underlying mantra for both these ideologies is: "Do not say anything that might upset someone."

Critical thinking is more difficult than most people think. It involves being vulnerable to the reality that we might be wrong in our initial opinion. And even worse, it involves the possibility that we may find ourselves with a different opinion than friends, fellow Christians, or family. For instance, even if we discover that objective data shows that Ford builds the best truck in the industry (purely a hypothetical illustration), most of us will still find it difficult to buy a Ford truck if our family always owned Chevy trucks, and our friends all drive Chevy trucks. This demonstrates the emotional side of critical thinking and the strong resistance we have to change.

There are several ways of looking at man's law and the command of 1 Peter 2:13 which says, "submit yourselves to every ordinance of man for the Lord's sake." Some see man's law as the final authority, and others see it as an authority that is itself subject to a higher authority or higher law. Here are two rather contemporary ways of looking at the law.

An individual who breaks a law that conscience tells him is unjust, and who willingly accepts the penalty of imprisonment in order to arouse the

conscience of the community over its injustice, is in
reality expressing the highest respect for the law.
Martin Luther King, Jr.

We always obeyed the law. Isn't that what
you do in America? Even if you don't agree
with a law personally, you still obey it.
Otherwise, life would be chaos.
Gertrude Scholtz-Klink, Chief of the Women's Bureau
under Reichsfuhrer Adolf Hitler, justifying her actions
during the holocaust.

As you can see, these are totally opposing perspectives on
man's law. Martin Luther King, Jr. saw the need for men to
abide by a higher law and consequently called laws that were
out of alignment with God's law unjust. Gertrude Scholtz-
Klink saw man's law as the final authority and claimed there
was no higher law to which mankind is accountable to obey
or acknowledge. She and many others attempted to use this
rationale to escape the charges of crimes against humanity at
the end of World War II.

I like the distinction John MacArthur makes concerning
the command "submit yourselves" (from a military term for
a soldier being under the authority of a superior). He notes
that we could also translate the term to read "put yourself in
an attitude of submission." The world would see this attitude as weak, but in reality it is harder to humbly submit to
punishment than it is to fight against an authority.

It was this attitude that caused John Bunyan, the author
of Pilgrim's Progress, to sit in jail for twelve years because
he refused to be licensed by the government to preach. It
was this attitude that caused Paul and Silas to be able to sing
in jail and allowed many martyred saints to pray for their
captors as they were being put to death.

What hinders us from being able to use unbridled objectivity when we consider the issue of civil disobedience? What should our relationship be to civil authority?

The best time to decide how we should respond to a potential problem is before the problem occurs. As Christians we need to have a platform anchored on secure biblical reality when the storms of persecution come.

The Fear of Controversy

There are at least three reasons why we find it so difficult to arrive at an objective biblical opinion on the subject of civil disobedience. The first is that it raises uncomfortable controversy. We, as human beings, find it difficult to change and generally avoid controversy. We have seen jail as a place for bad people, and we have seen Christians as good people. Often our fear is that if a Christian goes to jail, it will make other Christians look like bad people and raise controversy.

In reality, jail is not a place for bad people. Jail is a place that the authorities put people that they believe are bad people. When the authorities are following biblical standards of right and wrong, we can assume that only those who do wrong are in jail. However, when the authorities are not using biblical standards to judge right and wrong, it is very possible for good people to end up in jail. Remember the words of Voltaire, "It is dangerous to be right in matters on which the established authorities are wrong."

In order to objectively look at the Scriptures concerning the issue of civil disobedience and Christians going to jail, we must discard our assumptions. There are times and situations where good people, like John Bunyan, are imprisoned for doing what is right. Jesus and his followers have always been surrounded with controversy, and that controversy may be a good thing if it causes people to think and brings them face-to-face with biblical truth.

The Influence of Media Bias

The second reason that a majority of Christians separate themselves from Christians who have practiced civil disobedience is because they are interpreting everything through the eyes of a fallen world. You have heard it said that you cannot believe everything you read in the newspaper or see on television. Well, the truth is, you cannot believe <u>most</u> of what you read and see in the mainline media today.

The tendency for people to filter an event through their own presuppositions is normal. For instance, when we were remodeling an old country church in Swanville, Maine to make better use of the building for a growing congregation, I wrote of the event in a very positive fashion in letters to friends and in articles for our ministry newsletter. There were a few people in town that saw the same event in a negative way. They saw an old familiar building being changed. The story they would have written would have been one about uncaring and thoughtless destruction. The people doing this would have been described as selfish vandals of one of the town's prized landmarks, even though we took great care to maintain the original décor and appearance of the building. If you were exposed to only the negative report you would have a hard time defending those who were doing the destruction.

In 1990 Congressman Bob Dornan came to Binghamton, New York to speak at one of my fund-raiser dinners and to show his support of my state assembly campaign. The reporter that the paper sent to cover the event was clearly biased in her views on abortion, women's rights, and other liberal topics. She had a photographer with her that shot at least two rolls of film that night, half of which were taken of Congressman Dornan while he was speaking.

The next morning, the Press and Sun Bulletin ran her story. The story started out with, "Is there anything Bob

Dornan does not have an opinion about?" From that point on it went downhill. The facts about the event were never given, and it painted a picture of a radical right-wing boot camp. The article was accompanied by the most outlandish, contorted picture of Bob Dornan that could be found in two rolls of film. The reader would have no idea this was a well attended, upscale fund-raising banquet for a candidate running for the 124th NYS Assembly.

After contacting Bernie Griffin, the publisher, we both agreed that the article would be better suited for the Opinion page rather than the front page. He allowed me to write an unedited guest opinion to correct the problem. Fact is, most of the front page articles we read concerning controversial topics ought to be printed in the Opinion section. The cultural bias against evangelical Christianity found in most reporters makes it very difficult for them to write an objective report of a Christian activity that opposes what they believe.

The problem this creates is that the picture being painted by the article does not represent the actual event or the people involved. People reading the article assume that it must be accurate or they could not print it. This can have a huge impact within the church family.

Newspaper stories about me in the Binghamton, New York area affected how fellow Christians viewed me. On one occasion I was visiting the director of Arrowhead Bible Camp near Binghamton. The camp was hosting a Valentine dinner, and people were gathering in a game room outside the dining hall. Holly Pichura, a young lady who often worked at the camp, was attending the banquet and was shocked that I was at a Christian camp! She had seen my picture in the paper, read the stories of my being arrested, and concluded that I was not a Christian. She was really confused when her mother told her I was coming to their house to a meet-the-candidate event she was hosting for me. She later said, "I couldn't believe an ex-con was coming to our house!"

She eventually got to know me, and we are now best of friends. As a matter of fact, her name is now Holly Evans. She is the wife of our son Nathan and mother of our two grandsons, Kyler and Zachary. She learned that the media and the controversy they promote are untrustworthy sources of facts.

Former CNN anchor Aaron Brown gave a speech in Palm Beach at an event sponsored by Florida's Society of the Four Arts, and according to the <u>Palm Beach Daily News</u>, he didn't have very nice things to say about the news industry including: "Truth no longer matters in the context of politics and, sadly, in the context of cable news."

The real problem for the Christian community is that it has few reliable sources of information about current events. Christian people are portrayed in the secular media as unruly and lacking in character, and then we are asked if we agree with them. If we had factual information we would be better prepared to answer that question.

A reporter covering the Wichita, Kansas anti-abortion demonstrations for the Associated Press watched as Christians crawled on their hands and knees to sit in front of an abortion clinic where the police were already standing. They were seated several feet in front of the officers and would open up a path as officers wanted to leave or return to their posts. The headlines that day read, "Anti-abortion Protestors Storm Medical Clinic Pinning Police Officers to Fence." When I asked the reporter to justify his reporting of that morning, he said he changed the word "stormed" to "rushed" in the second release. Neither of these words gave an accurate picture of what took place. All across America, including my hometown, the image of violent, disrespectful thugs rushing a medical facility was given as accurate news coverage from Wichita. Then the question: "What do you think of those anti-abortion protesters down in Wichita?"

Paralyzed by Financial Pressures

The third reason it is hard to be an objective critical thinker on the topic of civil disobedience is because donor based organizations, including the church, believe the controversy surrounding civil disobedience will often affect contributions. As was stated earlier, our family lost 95% of our income when I became controversial in my attempt to participate in what I believed the Lord was doing through the churches in the Buffalo, New York area.

This is a sad but real problem. We are often placed in the uncomfortable position of realizing that our financial security, we believe and fear, will be put in jeopardy if we support or participate in that which is presently unpopular. The donors, the constituents, or the members are all voters in abstention when leaders consider issues of a controversial nature in most churches or Christian organizations. We profess to do our business before an audience of One, but the reality is that we are often swayed by the potential financial issues that could arise from our decisions. As a side note, God did have to redirect his support of our family through other channels when we became too controversial. The channels of our support have changed over the years, but the Source of our support has never changed. God is faithful to honor those who honor Him.

Controversy, media bias, and financial fears lie at the heart of the inability to objectively discuss civil disobedience and the Christian response to those in authority.

What does the Bible say about Civil Authority?

Whenever we consider a confrontation with civil authorities, we are reminded in the Scriptures that God has ordained them. Romans chapter 13 is one of the most commonly used Scriptures when the topic of civil authority is discussed. The first two verses say:

Let every person be in subjection to the governing authorities. For there is no authority except from God, and those which exist are established by God. Therefore he who resists authority has opposed the ordinance of God; and they who have opposed will receive condemnation upon themselves.

At first reading this verse appears to stand in opposition to any form of civil disobedience on the part of a Christian. However, this key passage actually limits the actions not only of individual citizens but also the actions of government. It makes both the civil authorities and the individual citizen subject to God and to a higher authority. The passage goes on to say,

For rulers are not a cause of fear for good behavior, but for evil. Do you want to have no fear of authority? Do what is good, and you will have praise from the same; for it is a minister of God to you for good. But if you do what is evil, be afraid; for it does not bear the sword for nothing; for it is a minister of God, an avenger who brings wrath upon the one who practices evil.

The passage limits individuals involved in civil disobedience because it reminds us that God ordained that the civil authorities carry the responsibility to punish evil and have been granted the sword to accomplish their mission. Individuals have not been given the responsibility to punish evil doers nor to take up the sword. Therefore, when we speak of civil disobedience we are not condoning bombing abortion clinics, shooting abortionists, or taking the law into our own hands.

Because it tells us that that the authorities bear the sword, it implies that there will be a price to pay for civil disobedience and we should be prepared to pay it.

The same verse that limits the actions of the citizen convicts the civil authorities concerning their responsibility before God. They are to protect good people and punish evil. When evil invades a society, the civil authorities, who are the enforcers of society's agenda, often abuse their God given authority. This puts the Christian in the middle of two authorities. One is the civil authority, which no longer accepts God's authority or His Word, and the other is God's authority as presented in His Word.

Did People Practice Civil Disobedience in the Bible?

The Bible is full of conflicts between God's people and the civil authorities. The thing we should look at is how these clashes were handled and what examples we are given.

In Exodus 1:17, the King of Egypt ordered the Hebrew midwives to kill all of the Hebrew newborn boys. They disobeyed the order of the king. They practiced civil disobedience every time they delivered a Hebrew boy and let him live. They refused to participate in the aborting of new-born children. What was their motive? The passage says, "But the midwives feared God and did not do as the King of Egypt had commanded them."

In 1 Samuel 19:1-2, Saul told his son Jonathan and his servants to kill David. Jonathan disobeyed and warned David instead. Saul was the civil authority, and he was being disobeyed. Jonathan confronted his father, the King, with these words, "Do not let the king sin against his servant David, since he has not sinned against you, and since his deeds have been very beneficial to you. For he took his life in his hand and struck the Philistine, and the LORD brought about a great deliverance for all Israel; you saw it and rejoiced. Why then will you sin against innocent blood, by putting David to death without a cause?" Notice that Jonathan reminded the King that God is the ultimate authority, and it is foolish to sin against God. This situation ended up with the civil authority recanting of his first order and allowing David to live. Sometimes civil disobedience gives the authorities an opportunity to rethink their position and do what is right.

In Daniel 3:1-18, King Nebuchadnezzar commanded three young men to bow down to a golden statue of him. The men refused and were thrown into a fiery furnace. What was the attitude of these three young men? Were they defiant toward civil authority? The account of the event says, "O Nebuchadnezzar, we do not need to give you an answer concerning this matter. If it be so, our God whom we serve is able to deliver us from the furnace of blazing fire; and He will deliver us out of your hand, O king. But even if He does not, let it be known to you, O king, that we are not going to serve your gods or worship the golden image that you have set up." Notice they showed respect to the King, but they lived before an audience of "One" and refused to bow down and worship any other god.

In Acts 5:40-42, the Sanhedrin set out to make an example of the apostles. Here is the account of the controversy. They called the apostles into the court room, flogged them, and ordered them to speak no more in the name of Jesus. They were released on their own recognizance. So they went on their way from the presence of the Council, rejoicing that they had been considered worthy to suffer shame for His Name. And everyday, in the temple and from house to house, they kept right on teaching and preaching Jesus as the Christ. Notice that they took their licking and kept on ticking. They recognized that preaching Jesus in a world that hates Him was going to be costly.

What about Jesus?

If there was ever a person who walked on this earth that understood how to obey God, it was Jesus. He was the One who established civil authority, and yet he was executed by the civil authority as a civil dissident. Here is what is recorded concerning his pre-sentencing negotiations. In John 19 we read:

> Pilate therefore said to Him, "You do not speak to me? Do You not know that I have authority to release You, and I have authority to crucify You?" Jesus answered, "You would have no authority over Me, unless it had been given you from above; for this reason he who delivered Me up to you has the greater sin." As a result of this Pilate made efforts to release Him, but the Jews cried out, saying, "If you release this Man, you are no friend of Caesar; everyone who makes himself out to be a king opposes Caesar."

This scene is very familiar to me. As a negotiator with civil authorities for Operation Rescue, I would see the same scenario unfold. Civil authorities often operate autonomously to suppress issues and problems. They are quick to remind you that they are the authority and can do as they please. When they are challenged about their God given role and shown that what they are doing is not right, many will try to do what is right. However, there is always someone else to whom one must answer who may have a different opinion. In this case, Pilate was intimidated by the thought of upsetting Caesar. In modern cases, it is often the intimidation of lawsuits and political punishment for failing to uphold an unjust law.

Take note of the interesting phrase, "for this reason he who delivered Me up to you has committed the greater sin." Many times civil authorities are put in a moral predicament by society's values and the current struggles. I have met many civil authorities who are pro-life or have pro-Christian values who would have liked to release us but hear the threats of a godless society ordering them to do their job. Jesus refused to say that Pilate was innocent in this issue, but He did remind him that society had gone the wrong way and was more to blame. Many policemen, judges, and other authorities are in an awkward place. In their heart they want to do what is right, but for fear of reprisal they remain the puppets of a godless society.

In Conclusion

The Bible does not encourage civil disobedience. It does, however, demonstrate that it is impossible to always obey a fallen civil authority and still walk with integrity before God. Fear of controversy, the influence of media bias, and financial pressures are real, but the call to obey God rather than man is also real.

We are called to honor all authorities. We are called to pray for those who despitefully use us. We are called to live at peace with all men if it is at all possible. However, we are called to fear God and God alone.

Pilate suffered a cold slap of reality when he was told that if he released Jesus he was no friend of Caesar. We face a cold slap of reality when we read in James 4:4 that friendship with the world is hostility toward God. Civil disobedience is something we should attempt to avoid, but there are times when, in order to obey God, we must disobey the civil authorities. Great heroes of the faith have been found cast into prisons and burned at the stake because an intolerant, totalitarian, civil authority demanded complete allegiance.

The day is already upon us when we will have to make unpopular decisions that will put us at odds with society. It may be at work, in the marketplace, or in our homes. It could be before a judge or in the midst of a crowd of hecklers. It is time for the American Christian to do some critical thinking about God's desire for us to obey Him rather than man.

RESPONDING IN CONFIDENCE

*"And now, Lord, take note of their threats,
and grant that Thy bond-servants
may speak Thy word
with all confidence"*

Acts 4:29a

CHAPTER FOUR

Responding in Confidence

—⟋⟍—

Faith-based Confidence

In the preceding chapters we looked at the culture we currently face in America and some of the Biblical issues that arise from living in post-Christian America. We cannot control the culture, but we can change our response to it. We have seen many times where a proper Christian response to a situation has allowed God to impact the situation and to glorify His Name. There are other times that God has allowed His children to suffer and even be martyred to declare His judgment on the wicked and to glorify His Name. The problem we often face is that we try to do what only God can do and neglect to do what is expected of us. It is God's responsibility and privilege to change things and judge the wicked. It is our responsibility to respond like Christians to situations and the wicked.

Consider the confidence of Daniel, the young Hebrew men who experienced the furnace, Paul during his beatings and imprisonment, and a host of other saints who responded with confidence in God even though they were uncertain of their circumstances and their accusers. Our response must be founded in confidence in order for our faith to be manifested to a faithless world. Look at the confidence of Stephen as he was being stoned to death for his faithful lifestyle of worship and witness. It appeared as though he lost everything. He did not live to preach another day, and yet his testimony has long outlived his short time on earth.

A young boy named Saul saw the face of Stephen as he stood by the coats of the religious men who were killing the Christian preacher. Later this young boy turned into a zealous crusader for Judaism. In the midst of his attempt to stamp out Christianity, he was confronted by the Lord and asked, "Why do you continue to persecute me?" I am convinced that the confidence and peace manifested in Steven haunted him as he carried out his hollow acts of religious piety. It is quite certain that what he saw in Stephen's face was reinforced over and over in the faces of other martyrs as he persecuted and killed Christians. Our confident response in spite of threatening circumstances is a message the world cannot deny.

Public Confidence

Our confidence must be in God and His Word alone. We cannot put confidence in the same things in which the world puts confidence. The world trusts money, power, politics, and security. These are the things they turn to when they are threatened. As Christians we cannot compromise God's Word in order to gain money, power, or large numbers of supporters.

This is why the "take back the culture" agenda has been virtually powerless. The fact is that we never owned our culture. Christians often fall prey to the illusion that the politicians and majorities control the American culture, but in reality they are merely a barometer of the American culture. They are not controlling the American culture, but their self-centered desire to stay in office, their hypocritical attempt to please the religious right, and their attempt to hold the party base by dancing around controversial issues represents the

American culture. Truth be known, we are all amateur politicians trying to win acceptance by those around us while attempting to carryout our desired agenda.

I have been in the back room of several campaign headquarters, including my own. I have been trained at the Republican candidate school in Washington, D.C. where I was taught that the only thing that cannot be compromised is winning the election. Because of this underlying corruption of our political system, we are generally restricted to voting for the better of two bad choices. This does not mean that we are relieved from the responsibility to apply salt to our culture on Election Day by casting our vote. It means that we must become wiser in our voting and recognize it is God who raises up the leaders of a nation to accomplish His purposes. Choose the person with the platform that best represents the moral demands of the Bible rather than the greedy demands of your wallet. Social security, lower taxes, and a host of other political hot buttons are vain hopes if God is not pleased with our moral actions.

What about motivating the masses and moving the culture through majority pressure? Large numbers of people, by God's grace, are capable of influencing and even making temporary changes. By this I mean changes that are headed in the right direction but soon to be overturned by a tyrannical judicial system. We are surrounded by groups that have specific agendas. We are told we must be an ally of a certain group in order to see our agenda stand a chance of winning. Politics, we are told, is all about the art of compromise. Being a God-fearing Christian has nothing to do with compromise.

As Francis Schaeffer said in his book <u>The Church at the End of the 20th Century</u>, we must distinguish between allies and co-belligerents. We may agree that certain people are saying the right thing about a certain issue but that does not mean we are allies with them. It merely means that we are agreeing with their opinion on that issue thus becoming co-belligerents with them. If we believe that our culture is at the mercy of the majority, then we will compromise Truth and become a member of a camp or group that has the numbers that cause us to feel powerful.

Does this mean that I support the separatist movement that not only abandons the marketplace debate in our culture but also divides the Body of Christ through pharisaical nit-picking? Absolutely not! We need to stand only on revealed Truth and allow it to be the Judge of all mankind.

I ran for political office carrying the Republican, Conservative, and Right-to-Life lines on my ballot. This means that I was viewed as being a member of each of these camps with all the images and reputations attributed to them. Actually I did not fit comfortably into any of them. There was an ongoing tension because I had difficulty overlooking certain subjects that I thought should be re-evaluated in light of Truth. The Republican Party had walked off the party plank decades before, the conservatives championed smaller government but were generally pro-abortion, the Right-to-Life party was willing to compromise theological truth for the sake of unity. I was co-belligerent with each of these groups in certain areas but also wanted to engage them in other positions that appeared to contradict revealed Truth.

Focused Confidence

Our confidence must rest squarely on the fact that God is at work in the affairs of man, and our only obligation is to obey Him and put the outcome in His hands. When we are focused on God we live lives that are hard to explain in natural terms. When our focus is on the circumstances that threaten us, we find ourselves responding as though we were totally on our own. Peter discovered this principle in the following situation.

And in the fourth watch of the night Jesus came to them, walking on the sea. And when the disciples saw Him walking on the sea, they were frightened, saying, "It is a ghost!" And they cried out for fear. But immediately Jesus spoke to them, saying, "Take courage, it is I; do not be afraid." And Peter answered Him and said, "Lord, if it is You, command me to come to You on the water." And He said, "Come!" And Peter got out of the boat, and walked on the water and came toward Jesus. But seeing the wind, he became afraid, and beginning to sink, he cried out, saying, "Lord, save me!" And immediately Jesus stretched out His hand and took hold of him, and said to him, "O you of little faith, why did you doubt?" Matt 14:25-31

We all have times of great confidence in the Lord. These are those special times when we lay aside our doubts and fears and do what we know the Lord has requested. It may be an act as simple as giving financial aid to a hurting person when we ourselves are financially challenged. Some have stepped out of the boat and opened their home to a girl in crisis with an unplanned pregnancy. Others have committed to tithing as a lifestyle.

Stepping out of the boat is an exciting experience. To rise above the natural circumstances of life that threaten us and to participate in a supernatural walk with the Lord is the utmost desire of true Christians. The problem arises when we begin to take our eyes off the Lord and place them on the precarious nature of our lives. As a young college student, I attended the annual mission conference at Calvary Independent Church in Lancaster, Pennsylvania. It was the highlight of my year to be engaged in such a large conference of both famous and little-known servants of God. Each year I met with an old missionary to China who was then a resident in the missionary retirement community in

Lancaster. He was a very tall man who was now hunched over with age. I often tried to imagine him as a tall, young missionary carrying the Gospel to the people of China. What a call God had placed on this man's heart! As we prayed together, his current passion for the Lord and ministry was still as fresh as it was when it dwelt inside a much younger body. He was heart broken for some of his friends who were retired from the field and living in the retirement home with him. He watched them become fearful and bitter to such a degree that it appeared as though they even denied the faith they had proclaimed for so many years.

Concerned that this would be his plight, he tried to figure out what had happened to his friends. Here is his conclusion. He said, "These people have served the Lord for many years and were always focused on the Lord, people, and the ministry. Now for the first time in their lives they are looking at their own mortality, aches, pains, and disappointments. What they are seeing is too much for them to bear, and they are sinking in the waves and circumstances of their lives. I have determined to keep my eyes on the Lord and the ministry He has for me. My field has changed, my body has changed, my circumstances have changed, but my Lord has not changed. This is how I plan to finish this race."

This is a very important principle. In the fall of 2005 my friend and co-laborer, George Callister, and I went on a bicycle trip from Bangor, Maine to Dublin, Georgia to raise funds for the people of Haiti. We learned that when we came to obstacles on the road we had to focus on where we wanted to steer, and look away from the threatening object. It seemed that our bicycle followed our focus. The same is true of our lives. Being a former drug addict, I have often counseled other addicts to focus on where they want to be instead of what they are attempting to get away from or avoid.

Lot was drawn to a lifestyle of compromise and sin when he gazed (focused) on the cities of Sodom and Gomorrah.

I do not know if it was the types of homes they had, the kind of chariots they drove, or their apparent prosperity. The Scriptures say it reminded him of Egypt. It is amazing that when you and I as Christians get focused on the world and its stuff, we forget what life in Egypt is really like. Soon we pitch our tents near, but not too near, the world from which we were called. Sometimes it is the lure of the world that gets our focus and distracts us from the course to which God has called us in His Son. Other times it is the threats and intimidations of the world that get our attention and cause us to waver in our faith.

In the Scriptures we see James writing to a group of converted Jews who were being persecuted, scattered, and intimidated by their culture. This passage of Scripture has had a profound influence on my life. This was the first book of the Bible that I listened to on tape. I remember the day like it was yesterday. I was sitting back in my old recliner listening to the hiss of the leader on the cassette tape passing over the heads on my newly purchased portable cassette player. Suddenly the booming voice of Alexander Scourby said,

My brethren, count it all joy when ye fall into diverse temptations. Knowing this, that the trying of your faith worketh patience. But let patience have her perfect work, that ye may be perfect and entire, wanting nothing. If any of you lack wisdom, let him ask of God, who giveth to all men liberally, and upbraideth not, and it shall be given him. But let him ask in faith, nothing wavering. For he that wavereth is like a wave of the sea driven with the wind and tossed. For let not that man think that he shall receive anything of the Lord. A double-minded man is unstable in all his ways. James 1:2-8 KJV

God tells us that when the whole world seems to be against us we should rejoice, because our faith is being tested, and the testing will increase our patience and maturity to the point that we will have contentment. We are to have confidence in times of calamity and courage in times of danger. To focus on God's work in our lives and not the negative circumstances that threaten us is our challenge. There is no need to be tossed by the waves or to sink when problems, trials, and tribulations lap at our feet.

Casting Crowns sings a song that speaks about this battle we have with wanting to be confident Christians and seeing the reality of the world's intimidation. Consider the words of the first verse:

Oh what I would do to have
The kind of faith it takes
To climb out of this boat I'm in
Onto the crashing waves
To step out of my comfort zone
Into the realm of the unknown where Jesus is
And He's holding out His hand
But the waves are calling out my name
And they laugh at me
Reminding me of all the times
I've tried before and failed
The waves they keep on telling me
Time and time again. "Boy, you'll never win!"
"You'll never win!"

Chorus:
But the voice of truth tells me a different story
The voice of truth says, "Do not be afraid!"
The voice of truth says, "This is for My glory"
Out of all the voices calling out to me
I will choose to listen and believe the voice of truth

When troubles come there are many voices that call out to us. There are suggestions from some from well meaning yet shallow Christians, others from worldly sources, and then there is the impulse of our own flesh, which usually reacts in a selfish way. If we are willing to listen, the Holy Spirit and the Word of God will present the Truth to us for our wisdom and comfort.

We must lay hold of the faith spoken of in the eleventh chapter of Hebrews. We need to understand that it is the substance of things hoped for, the evidence of things not yet seen. It was by this faith and confidence that men of old gained approval. It is by this faith we understand that the worlds were prepared by the Word of God, so that what is seen was not made out of things which are visible. The very waves that intimidated Peter were made by God. When Jesus told them to be calm, they were calm. The very people and circumstances that threaten us are likewise subject to God's control.

Intelligent Confidence

Francis Bacon was right when he said, "A little science estranges a man from God. A lot of science brings him back." Stanley L. Miller in a report published by NASA in 1996 stated that mathematicians, with the aid of computers, have simulated Darwinian chance models of evolution over billions of years. The outcome showed that the probability of evolution through chance processes was zero, no matter how long the time scale.

Sir Fred Hoyle, famous astronomer, says the evolution by chance process is, "equivalent to giving 10^{50} (10 with 50 zeros behind it) blind people a Rubiks cube and finding that they all solve the cube at the same moment."

We have no need to fear science but should embrace it as it discovers and uncovers the mysteries of God. We seem to be confident of God's truth when we are among Christians, but in the public marketplace we become silent and intimidated as though there are two sets of truths, one for Christians and one for the rest of the world. Evolution is false science. It is the genesis theory of the religion of Humanism. It serves as the theoretic explanation of the origin of all things that exist based on the presupposition that there is no God, no supernatural. From that unfounded assumption it attempts to explain the universe. When man rejects God he is left with no hope as he attempts to explain what his blindness can not see.

It is hard to have a response based on confidence when it appears as though the whole world is against you. Paul, the apostle, faced a hostile world, but he knew why things were the way they were. The Roman Empire was every bit as corrupt and threatening as the world around us today. In his letter to the saints living in the heart of the empire, Paul wanted them to know that he was aware of the decadent culture but was confident of the reality of God. If you look around you can see that God has revealed Himself to His children and to the world. Meditate on what God's Word tells us about his view of mankind, and then consider how this should impact our daily lives.

Romans 1:16-32 is a commentary on our culture that was written thousands of years ago. I have included this lengthy section of Scripture so that you can understand why things are the way they are. Once you and I understand the situation, we can move forward with confidence. I have added some comments within the text.

> For I am not ashamed of the gospel, for it is the power of God for salvation to everyone who believes, to the Jew first and also to the Greek. For in it the righteousness of God is revealed from faith to faith; as it is written, "But the righteous man shall live by faith." (*Note: Paul has confidence in God because of the power of the work of salvation and the righteousness of God that is revealed in all those who believe.*

There is no natural explanation for the life-changing power of the Gospel. Paul experienced it personally and witnessed it often.)

For the wrath of God is revealed from heaven against all ungodliness and unrighteousness of men, who suppress the truth in unrighteousness, because that which is known about God is evident within them; for God made it evident to them. For since the creation of the world His invisible attributes, His eternal power and divine nature, have been clearly seen, being understood through what has been made, so that they are without excuse. *(Note: Deep down in the recesses of every human being there is an acknowledgment of God. It may not be defined, but the soul knows there is more to life than what we see. Notice that there is an agenda to suppress the Truth in unrighteousness.)*

For even though they knew God, they did not honor Him as God, or give thanks; but they became futile in their speculations, and their foolish heart was darkened. *(Note: The inability of the unregenerate person to understand is not something they choose but is a result of their rejection of God. I find it sad that we are often intimidated by sincere people whose hearts are blind, and who can only offer foolish speculations.)* Professing to be wise, they became fools, and exchanged the glory of the incorruptible God for an image in the form of corruptible man and of birds and four-footed animals and crawling creatures.

Therefore God gave them over in the lusts of their hearts to impurity, that their bodies might be dishonored among them. For they exchanged the truth of God for a lie, and worshiped and served the creature rather than the Creator, who is blessed forever. Amen. *(Note: The elevation of animals to human status and the lowering of human life to the status of animals is evidence of a mind devoid of true wisdom and warped as a result.)*

For this reason God gave them over to degrading passions; for their women exchanged the natural function for that which is unnatural, and in the same way also the men abandoned the natural function of the woman and burned in their desire toward one another, men with men committing indecent acts and receiving in their own persons the due penalty of their error. *(Note: Homosexuality is a degrading passion with personal consequences. If we had any compassion at all, we would be reaching out to the homosexual community with love and a desire to free them from the bondage of this horrible sin.)*

And just as they did not see fit to acknowledge God any longer, God gave them over to a depraved mind, to do those things which are not proper, being filled with all unrighteousness, wickedness, greed, evil; full of envy, murder, strife, deceit, malice; they are gossips, slanderers, haters of God, insolent, arrogant, boastful, inventors of evil, disobedient to parents, without understanding, untrustworthy, unloving, unmerciful; and, although they know the ordinance of God, that those who practice such things are worthy of death, they not only do the same, but also give hearty approval to those who practice them. (Note: *How close does this come to describing what is taking place in our culture?)*

In the middle of writing this book I found myself between ministries and working in a sales position at a local resort. This was the first time I had worked full-time outside of ministry in many years. It was an eye-opener in several ways. First of all, I saw how our culture has demonstrated the truthfulness of Romans chapter one. I am far from naïve, but I was shocked at the casual attitude toward what was considered repulsively scandalous just a few years ago. Secondly, I experienced the tremendous pressure to not condemn and to even blend into the culture.

Several people attempted to edit some of their language and subject matter when speaking to me. Some began to use religious concepts and sincerely speak of prayer and God. This experience gave me a new burden for the lost. Many know that what they are doing is wrong or why would they attempt to correct it in front of me. Some are being totally destroyed by sin and yet refuse to place the blame for their dilemma on their personal lifestyle and choices.

I can understand how the aggressiveness and apparent confidence our culture manifests may cause us to lose heart or to lack confidence in our response to its claims. However, it is a sad thing that Christians are intimidated by people plagued by foolish speculation who have had their hearts darkened and have been given over to a depraved mind. Instead, we should have compassion on them and a desire to see them made alive in Christ and set free from sin.

The issues of life are all based on our understanding of how life began. If we fail to acknowledge that God created what we see, then we are destined to operate in the dark with foolish speculation as our best shot, i.e. evolution. If we understand that God created everything that exists, then we can deal with life's issues in the context of God's power and presence.

Moral Confidence

There is nothing Christ-like about compromising morality for social acceptance. There are things that are wrong, and there are consequences to doing what is wrong. Remember what Jesus said about living a life within the confines of morality. "Enter by the narrow gate; for the gate is wide, and the way is broad that leads to destruction, and many are those who enter by it. For the gate is small, and the way is narrow that leads to life, and few are those who find it." (Matthew 7:13,14)

This truth had its roots back in the Old Testament as it warned; "There is a way which seems right to a man, but its end is the way of death." (Proverbs 14:12) Remember, man is blind. His judgment, by nature, is blurred at best. When it comes to morality it does not matter if the majority is practicing what the Bible declares wrong; it remains wrong.

The Christian who acknowledges that there are moral absolutes and that those absolutes are found in the Bible is not being judgmental but rather being truthful. He himself is judged by the same standards. Having moral convictions is not a judgment of people, but it is a judgment of certain behavior. We must have confidence in the moral standards of the Bible and apply them first to ourselves then to the church. God will apply them to those outside the church. Oh, how we reverse this principle. We are quick to judge the world but find it hard to practice discipline within the church. This is an important issue that some have ignored, failing to understand it is the plain teaching of Scripture. Consider what 1 Corinthians 5:9-13 says:

> I wrote you in my letter not to associate with immoral people; I did not at all mean with the immoral people of this world, or with the covetous and swindlers, or with idolaters; for then you would have to go out of the world. But actually, <u>I wrote to you not to associate with any so-called brother if he should be an immoral person, or covetous, or an idolater, or a reviler, or a drunkard, or a swindler — not even to eat with such a one.</u> For what have I to do with judging outsiders? Do you not judge those who are within the church? But those who are outside, God judges.

Remove the wicked man from among yourselves.
Emphasis mine.

If we had enough confidence in the moral standards in the Bible to apply them to the Christian community, the world may even begin to consider their validity.

The world says that divorce is better than unhappy people in a marriage. The world says that homosexuality is a personal orientation that is as natural and right as hetero-sexuality. The world says there are no absolutes and that ethics change with the situation. The world says that people who call these things sin are hate mongers and intolerant bigots. How many professing Christians agree with these statements? How many are intimidated by this logic?

In our flesh some of what the world is saying seems right. But if it contradicts the revealed Word of God then it is wrong. The sins pointed out in the Bible are still sins and still have the consequences of sin. We will deal more with this topic in the next chapter.

Heavenly Confidence

It has been said by some that Christians can be so heav-enly minded that they are no earthly good. I disagree with this statement. I know that the Christian can be so earthly minded that he is no heavenly good. We often live as though this is the only life that we have. We live as though eter-nity was not ours. This character flaw manifests itself in many ways. It can manifest itself in our lifestyles. We lay up treasures on earth as though they are the goal of our lives. When thieves break in and steal them or when moths and rust destroy them, as Jesus said would happen, we act as if it is the end of the world. We occupy ourselves with keeping up with the Jones' and fail to keep up with Jesus. We have more confidence in the things we can see than we do in the things God has told us. Consider this passage in Hebrews

11, the great Hall of Faith. I have added some notes within the context.

> All these died in faith, without receiving the promises, but having seen them and having welcomed them from a distance, and having confessed that they were strangers and exiles on the earth. *(Note: These people were heavenly minded and had a heavenly confidence.)* For those who say such things make it clear that they are seeking a country of their own. And indeed if they had been thinking of that country from which they went out, they would have had opportunity to return. *(Note: We are called out of the darkness into His wonderful kingdom of light. See 1 Peter 2:9. These saints never paid attention to the kingdom of darkness from which they had been called but sought first the Kingdom of God.)* But as it is, they desire a better country that is a heavenly one. Therefore God is not ashamed to be called their God; for He has prepared a city for them. Heb 11:13-16

The last sentence in that section intrigues me. Could it be that God is ashamed of us when we live as though we have no hope beyond this life? Consider Sir Michael Faraday, a great scientist and Christian man, who was questioned on his death bed by journalists concerning his speculations about life after death. He responded, "Speculations, I know nothing of speculations. I am resting on certainties. I know that my Redeemer lives and because He lives, I live also." As a pastor I have been at the bedside of dying people. I have witnessed the difference between those who have a confident faith and those who cleave only to this world.

Pastor Bob Roberts, one of my closest friends, was one of the most inquisitive Christians I knew. He and I would spend hours measuring and probing the mysteries of God. One day he was diagnosed with terminal pancreatic cancer. Although the circumstances of his life changed, his passion to know more of Christ never ceased. I had the privilege of spending several days with him as his physical life came to an end. Throughout the night watches we would ponder Scripture and find rest for our spirits in the great hymns of the faith. Bob passed from this life to the next without a flinch because the road upon which he walked always reached beyond this life. Passing beyond the veil of this existence merely meant a complete revelation of the mysteries his heart longed to understand. His heavenly confidence was an earthly witness to the world and a blessing to the Christian hospice nurses and others who worshipped the God of Life when they made their visit to Bob's chapel on his death bed.

Throughout history God's people have worshipped and demonstrated confidence beyond the grave as they faced the valley of the shadow of death. Worship and confidence are undeniable marks of the martyrs. In a less spectacular way, they are the ministry of every believer as he or she bids farewell to this fallen existence and anticipates the presence of the Lord. It has been said that the reality of a man's faith can be better seen in the hour of his death than in the totality of his life on earth. A person who has overcome the fear of death is a person who is truly free to live.

The Christian has hope that goes beyond any circumstance, beyond any struggle, and even beyond the grave itself. It is a heavenly confidence that contradicts logic and pulls us ever forward toward our ultimate place in glory.

We are to give an answer for the hope that lies within us, and yet it would seem from our anxiety, fear, and uncertainty that we are as hopeless as the rest of the world. It has been my contention that we have been giving answers to people who have no reason to be asking questions.

Visible Confidence

How can people know that we are Christians? Is it the fish symbol on our minivan or the Bible in our backseat? Is it the style of clothes we wear or the length of our hair? Could it be the style of music we listen to or the places we go? Or perhaps which church we attend? No, no, no to all these. It is by our lifestyle that we are known to be different. Our lifestyle includes many dynamics, but one of them is our confidence in the face of life's issues.

Consider the mark of Christianity that people saw in Peter and John. Peter and John were arrested for publicly proclaiming the resurrection from the dead through Jesus. Under normal circumstances in the pantheistic Roman Empire, teaching a theoretic doctrine in the public streets was not cause for arrest. Why were these two arrested? Acts 4:11-12 is the reason for the arrest. Peter and John were saying, "He (Jesus) is the stone which was rejected by you, the builders, but which became the chief cornerstone. And there is salvation in no one else; for there is no other name under heaven that has been given among men by which you must be saved." They were being very intolerant of the other religions in the empire.

I recently taught at a Christian university that was going through some re-focusing exercises. The administration wanted to clarify the worldview of the various schools in the university system. Each faculty member was given a copy of The Universe Next Door and was required to attend workshops on worldviews. The desire of the administration was to be sure that all the disciplines of the various schools at the university were being taught from a Christian worldview.

One afternoon, as I prepared for my evening class, I overheard a conversation in the hallway between two of my colleagues. They were very frustrated that the administration expected them to teach the Christian worldview as the only legitimate worldview. They felt that it was intolerant and academically narrow. If this is the mindset on a Christian campus, imagine what the non-Christian thinks of the exclusive claims of the true Gospel.

The same mindset existed in the Roman Empire at the time of Peter and John. Were Peter and John wrong? Were they intolerant and ignorant? Acts 4:13 tells us what impact their confidence had on the onlookers. It says: "Now as they observed the confidence of Peter and John and understood that they were uneducated and untrained men, they were amazed, and began to recognize them as having been with Jesus." They wore one of the marks of a Christian; confidence.

We must respond to life's issues with faith and confidence. This is different from responding with pride and arrogance. Pride and arrogance are reserved for religious Pharisees, of which there are far too many already. Our faith and confidence are in God and His Word. This can be best summed up with the conclusion of the situation Peter and John faced.

When they had been released, they went to their own companions and reported all that the chief priests and elders had said to them. And when they heard this, they lifted their voices to God with one accord and said, 'O lord, it is You who made the heaven and the earth and the sea, and all that is in them, Who by the Holy Spirit, through the mouth of our father David Your servant, said, 'Why did the Gentiles rage, and the peoples devise futile things? The kings of the earth took their stand, and the rulers were gathered together against the Lord and against His Christ.' For truly in this city there were gathered together against Your holy servant Jesus, whom You anointed, both Herod and Pontius Pilate, along with the Gentiles and the peoples of Israel, to do whatever Your hand and Your purpose predestined to occur. And now, Lord,

take note of their threats, and grant that Your bond-servants may speak Your Word with all confidence.
Acts 4:23-29

The controversy and situation brought unity to the believers. There was an understanding that God was the Creator God and that everything was His and nothing was out of His control. Knowing that God's Word is true, they quoted what God said about the enemy rising up against Christ and His servants. Believing God was at work, a present day application was made to God's Word, and He was asked to continue to give them confidence in their response to a threatening world.

Martin Luther lived in a threatening upside-down world. He was chased, persecuted, and ultimately excommunicated from the Catholic Church. He wrote "A Mighty Fortress is Our God" and lived the truths and hopes of what he found in the Scriptures. I enjoy and embrace one of his quotes about his outlook on life. In the midst of uncertainty and a threatening world he said, "Even if I knew that tomorrow the world would go to pieces, I would still plant my apple tree." Do not fail to plan for the future even when the future looks threatening. As one of my college professors would say, "Plan as though the Lord will not return for another hundred years. Live as though He is coming tomorrow."

"Lord, give us a response founded on confidence as we face life's issues and challenges."

RESPONDING IN INNOCENCE

*"Behold, I send you out as sheep
in the midst of wolves;
therefore be shrewd as serpents,
and innocent as doves."*

Matthew 10:16

CHAPTER FIVE

Responding in Innocence

—⚹—

Innocent but Accused

To be framed means to have a situation painted in such a way that it would appear as though you are guilty. It is usually the tool of the truly guilty person who attempts to avoid the consequences of his or her actions by making it look like someone else is guilty. The person who is framed must rely on the evidence to establish his or her innocence.

There is an old adage that goes something like this: If you were accused of being a Christian, would there be enough evidence to convict you? I would like to play off of that thought and ask, "If you were accused of being a liar, a drunkard, a fornicator, a gossip, a bigot, or a hypocrite, would there be enough evidence to clear you of the charges?" As Christ followers we will be accused of these things and more. If we are going to have a valid Christian response to the world, the evidence must prove us innocent.

It seems that the newspapers are full of scandals involving Christian leaders. These stories are used to damage the claims of Christianity. The world points a finger and says "You are not what you say you are, and you are not what you tell others to be, therefore you are a hypocrite, and anyone who believes what you believe is also a hypocrite." For those attempting to live godly lives, it seems as though all Christians are being framed because of the behavior of a few. This causes many to discredit the role that innocence plays in responding to a threatening world.

There is a difference between being accused and being innocent. Peter and John were accused of being bad guys who were trouble makers. In reality, the Truth was the trouble maker. Peter and John were innocent. Acts 4:21a says, "When they [the authorities] had threatened them further, they let them go, finding no basis on which to punish them . . ." Peter and John had done nothing wrong. In like manner, Pilate declared Jesus to be "a man with no guile." We must live our lives in such a way that we are found innocent in our character and behavior.

Innocence Convicts

Why does the world rejoice when one of God's people falls? Most of the events that become scandals in a Christian leader's life are commonplace in the lifestyle of the world. There was little fuss made as five different men stepped forward to claim that they fathered the child of Anna Nicole Smith. The world has come to accept infidelity, drug use, and other immoral behavior as normal, except in the life of a professed Christian. I believe there are two reasons for this paradox.

First of all, all mankind was made in the image of God, and there is a natural guilt that sin brings to every person. The defense mechanism for guilt is to justify the action through pointing to the failure of others, especially those who attempted to make you feel guilty. A professing Christian who falls into public sin gives others a short reprise from accusation and serves as a balm to their guilt. Remember Satan is "the accuser of the brethren." Look at what the angels say as he is cast down to the earth during the final days of God's prophesy. "Now the salvation, and the power, and the kingdom of our God and the authority of His Christ have come, for the accuser of our brethren has been thrown down, who accuses them before our God day and night." (Rev 12:10-11) The only hope the world has is for God's people to be wrong. When God's people fall, it gives the world some hope that the message they proclaim has fallen also.

Secondly, the world holds the Christian to a different standard than the rest of the world. After all, the Christian is the one with the moral measuring rod. He is the one who tells others how to live. When he teaches one thing and lives contrary to that teaching he naturally falls into judgment. James reminds us of this in chapter 3:1-2:

> Let not many of you become teachers, my brethren, knowing that as such we shall incur a stricter judgment. For we all stumble in many ways. If anyone does not stumble in what he says, he is a perfect man, able to bridle the whole body as well.

This verse could mean that we should avoid being teachers so we can stumble through life, or it can mean that as we mature in our walk we will be held to higher standards. The Bible supports the latter. We read in Hebrews 5:12-14:

> For though by this time you ought to be teachers, you have need again for someone to teach you the elementary principles of the oracles of God, and you have come to need milk and not solid food. For everyone who partakes only of milk is not accustomed to the word of righteousness, for he is a babe. But solid food is for the mature, who because of practice have their senses trained to discern good and evil.

You see, God expects us to mature and to become those teachers. What the verse is reminding us of is that as we grow in Christ and teach others about God, salvation, and sin we will be held to a higher standard.

It was the lifestyle of innocence that caused Joseph to spend time in jail as he was framed by the wife of his boss because he refused to commit sin with her. Throughout history those who refused to join the wicked became the target of the wrath of the wicked. Their decisions brought with them a degree of discomfort, but they also led to spiritual blessing and strength.

There are several ways to respond to threats and judgment. First, you can compromise your lifestyle and blend in with your culture at work or school. You will still be mocked as a hypocrite but probably behind your back. Secondly, you could totally distance yourself from your culture at work or school and just be that weird religious person that doesn't bother anyone. This will also protect you because it allows the lost to avoid the guilt of hearing the Truth. Or you could live a life of confidence, compassion, and innocence that God will honor and use to glorify His name. You may not be the most popular person for taking this position, but you will experience the blessing of God and will make an impact for eternity with your life.

Innocence is Liberating

We can expect to be accused. Remember Jesus said, "Blessed are you when men cast insults at you, and persecute you, and say all kinds of evil against you falsely, on account of Me. Rejoice, and be glad, for your reward in heaven is great, for so they persecuted the prophets who were before you." (Matt 5:11-12) When our life is framed in innocence, then we can have confidence as we stand before a threatening world.

In 1971, after spending twenty-seven months in Vietnam, I returned home as a heroin addict to a conservative area near Lancaster, Pennsylvania. Because I frequented family and friends who knew me before I went to Vietnam and new friends that were associated with my addiction, I was living as two people. My new lifestyle included guns, drugs, and a world that was radically counter-culture to everything around me. As I moved in and out of these two worlds for several years, I was afraid that my friends in the biker/drug world would lose confidence in me or that my family and old friends might disown me if they found out what I was doing and who I was associating with. Many Christians today are living in two worlds also. It may not be as bad as my situation was, but there is a definite difference in how they behave in each world.

One of the greatest things that came as a bonus to my salvation was that I no longer had anything to hide. For a while after I came to Christ I would have a momentary cringe when someone opened the console in my car, but then I would remember that there was nothing hidden there. There were no drugs, or guns, or paraphernalia as there might have been before my salvation. Innocence is liberating. One of the reasons Christians are boxed in is because they are lacking innocence. Paul chastened the Christians of his day for their lack of openness because of their compromised lives. He wrote,

> Our mouth has spoken freely to you, O Corinthians, our heart is opened wide. You are not restrained by us, but you are restrained in your own affections. Now in a like exchange — I speak as to children — open wide to us also.
>
> Do not be bound together with unbelievers; for what partnership have righteousness and lawlessness, or what fellowship has light with darkness? Or what harmony has Christ with Belial, or what has a believer in common with an unbeliever? 2 Corinthians 6:11-16

We become restrained when we attempt to live in two worlds. We are prisoners of our own making as Paul told the Corinthians. He was not causing them the stress they were experiencing in their Christian life; they were causing it themselves because of their affections. They had compromised lives and were not innocent.

Innocence Empowers

When we have nothing to hide, nothing to lose, and nothing to gain we become very powerful. Remember the dilemma that Daniel faced when he was accused of dishonoring the king. He continued to pray to God after an injunction had been issued that said anyone who prayed to any god but the king would be thrown into the lion's den. Daniel refused to rebel. He refrained from attacking the king for issuing the injunction. Instead he continued to practice his life of integrity before God and the king. The king was grieved that someone like Daniel would be caught in this snare of conspiracy. Listen to what Daniel said when the king came to check on his condition.

> Then Daniel spoke to the king, "O king, live forever! My God sent His angel and shut the lions' mouths, and they have not harmed me, *inasmuch as I was found innocent before Him*; and also toward you, O king, I have committed no crime." Dan 6:21-22 *Emphasis mine.*

Daniel had a life that was wide open for view. When his life was examined he was found to be innocent. While he was doing what God wanted him to do, God was at work doing what He wanted to do. Look at what follows:

> Then Darius the king wrote to all the peoples, nations, and men of every language who were living in all

the land: "May your peace abound! I make a decree that in all the dominion of my kingdom men are to fear and tremble before the God of Daniel. Daniel 6:25-26

I again would like to note that we are called to focus on our personal lives, and then God is free to deal with the culture. I disagree with the "take back the culture" agenda and am also unable to find a "hide out until Jesus comes" agenda anywhere in Scriptures. I do see God's people living lives that first honor God and then honor all men, living at peace with them as much as is possible.

Innocence is a liberating and powerful condition that is lacking in 21st century Christian life. By the world's standards we appear relatively good, but what about by God's standards? Notice Daniel's order when he evaluated his innocence. He said that he was found innocent before God and also toward the king.

When we read things like this our mind automatically evaluates the condition of the church. It is easy to say the church in America is not innocent before God, however we must remember that the testimony of the church is merely the combined testimonies of each of its professing members. We cannot hide out in the crowd and ignore our personal life before God. I am writing this book for readers like you who are Daniels wrestling with living meaningful Christian lives in a post-Christian culture.

For the remainder of this chapter on innocence I am going to touch on subjects that are commonplace in the church. We can no longer wink at the behavior of professing Christians that contradicts the clear teaching of God. You and I cannot justify such behavior in our personal lives just because it is no longer disciplined in the established church. Our lack of innocence deeply affects our Christian response.

Lack of Innocence Restrains our Response

If we are to have a Christian response to the world around us, then we must come to terms with some of the things that prevent us from being found innocent when the world inspects our lifestyle. For example, I was involved in some organizational planning in a local church. As I began to suggest specific people for specific tasks, I was made aware of all sorts of issues the church had to work around when working with its leaders. Some leaders were divorced from other leaders and still felt uncomfortable around each other. Some leaders were at odds with other leaders and could not work together. Some leaders were relatives of divorced people in the church and could not operate in close fellowship with them. I was aghast to say the least.

How can we tolerate strife, bitterness, gossip, divorce, and a host of other things in the church and in the lives of those who attain to be teachers? These folks were hindered in any opportunity to be open to one another. They still had things hidden in the compartments of their lives that prohibited them from experiencing the liberating empowerment of innocence.

Does this mean that only perfect people can be effective Christians and leaders? Not at all. Consider the life of Paul, the apostle, who called himself the chief of all sinners. We are hard pressed to live a perfect life, but we can live an open life that strives to be found innocent before God and man. The Scriptures are quick to remind us that if we say we have no sin, we are liars. But when we sin, we must confess it as sin and find forgiveness from a faithful God who will also cleanse us from all unrighteousness. The word translated "confess" in 1 John 1:9 is the Greek word "homologoomen" which literally means to say the same thing about our actions as God says. If we are to establish the cultural high-ground of innocence then we need to start saying the same thing about the issues in our lives as God says about them.

What does God say about divorce? Although it is far from my intention to write a thesis on the subject, we must reflect on the problem this practice is causing in the church. We know God permitted divorce because of the hardness of the hearts of people, but his standard is still anti-divorce, and this should be the standard of every God fearing Christian. Does divorce happen to Christians? Sure it does, but it should not happen with the same regularity that it does in the world. When it does happen, it should not happen without intervention of the church and without a struggle to prevent it at all costs.

Things should not be construed as better because of the divorce. Things are not better as children are shipped between parents like common property. Things are not better when girls have multiple father figures on the wedding day, and the consequences of the divorce mar the joy of the occasion. Things are not better when our children are taught by example that marriages are not permanent, and divorce is acceptable and in some cases preferred. 1 Corinthians 7:10-16 has some pretty plain instructions for married Christian people and for those who face the departure of an unsaved spouse. I have included comments within the text.

But to the married [Christians] I give instructions, not I, but the Lord, that the wife should not leave her husband (but if she does leave, let her remain unmarried, or else be reconciled to her husband), and that the husband should not send his wife away. *(Note: This seems pretty simple to understand. If both parties profess to be Christians then they can remain together or remain unmarried apart.)* But to the rest I say, not the Lord, *(Note: This does not make this any less the Word of God. It means that Paul is not quoting direct verbiage from God but is being led by the Holy Spirit. The condition of a new believer having an unbelieving spouse was an increasing and new issue as the Gospel went forward.)* that if any brother has a wife who is an unbeliever, and she consents to live with him, let him not send her away. And a woman who has an unbelieving husband, and he consents to live with her, let her not send her husband away. For the unbelieving husband is sanctified through his wife, and the unbelieving wife is sanctified through her believing husband; for otherwise your children are unclean, but now they are holy. *(Note: God sees the consequences of divorce on children. Remember when it was said, "Oh, they are just staying together because of the children." What is wrong with that? It seems a lot less selfish than what takes place when children become nothing more than shared marital assets.)* Yet if the unbelieving one leaves, let him leave; the brother or the sister is not under bondage in such cases, but God has called us to peace. *(Note: During the process of attempting to prevent a divorce, the church will find itself in a case of discipline. If there is no repentance during the process it must move forward. If it moves to the final act of discipline before the church, then the disciplined person is to be considered an unbeliever. (Matthew 18:15-20) Very few churches today call a couple to task for seeking a divorce. We have bought the lie of the world that it is a personal decision that is void of moral standards.)* For how do you know, O wife, whether you will save your husband? Or how do you know, O husband, whether you will save your wife?

What does God say directly about divorce? Malachi 2:13-16 is very clear. It could be that our churches are not experiencing the power of God because we are not innocent in this area.

> And this is another thing you do: you cover the altar of the LORD with tears, with weeping and with groaning, because He no longer regards the offering or accepts it with favor from your hand. Yet you say, "For what reason?" Because the LORD has been a witness between you and the wife of your youth, against whom you have dealt treacherously, though she is your companion and your wife by covenant. But not one has done so who has a remnant of the Spirit. And what did that one do while he was seeking a godly offspring? Take heed then, to your spirit, and let no one deal treacherously against the wife of your youth. For I hate divorce, says the LORD, the God of Israel, and him who covers his garment with wrong, says the LORD of hosts. So take heed to your spirit, that you do not deal treacherously.

Are you and I ready to "homologoomen" (say the same thing) about divorce as God says? God does not hate divorce merely because it is wrong. God hates divorce because of the pain and heartache it brings to His people in particular. He hates it because of how it smears the picture He has made to demonstrate the relationship he has with the Church.

> Wives, be subject to your own husbands, as to the Lord. For the husband is the head of the wife, as Christ also is the head of the church, He Himself being the Savior of the body. But as the church is subject to Christ, so also the wives ought to be to their husbands in everything. Husbands, love your wives, just as Christ also loved the church and gave Himself up for her; that He might sanctify her, having cleansed her

by the washing of water with the word, that He might present to Himself the church in all her glory, having no spot or wrinkle or any such thing; but that she should be holy and blameless. So husbands ought also to love their own wives as their own bodies. He who loves his own wife loves himself; for no one ever hated his own flesh, but nourishes and cherishes it, just as Christ also does the church, because we are members of His body. For this cause a man shall leave his father and mother, and shall cleave to his wife; and the two shall become one flesh. <u>This mystery is great; but I am speaking with reference to Christ and the church. Nevertheless let each individual among you also love his own wife even as himself; and let the wife see to it that she respect her husband.</u> (Ephesians 5:22-33) *(Emphasis mine.)*

Divorce is a sad reality in a fallen world, but it should be a rare and embarrassing occurrence among Christians.

There are other things that have also become commonplace. What about backbiting, gossiping, and hating? These are sins against other people. This is not a new problem. It is a human problem. It existed in the early church. When Paul was preparing to visit the church at Corinth, he was concerned that they were not prepared for his visit, and he would have to confront their sin. Here is what he wrote:

For I am afraid that perhaps when I come I may find you to be not what I wish and may be found by you to be not what you wish; that perhaps there may be strife, jealousy, angry tempers, disputes, slanders, gossip, arrogance, disturbances. 2 Corinthians 12:20

Note the list of things Paul did not want to find when he arrived. These are the very things that the world sees in many churches today. A church that preaches love, joy, and peace is full of strife, jealousy, and disputes. If you have children you know that it is hard to correct them if you are guilty of the same thing. It is hard to tell your children not to be mean to each other if they continually hear you tearing others down. It is hard to tell the world of the love of God when they do not see it in our lives. Our response is restrained and nullified because of our lack of innocence.

When There Is No Difference

George Barna, in a recent poll, found that only nine percent of all born-again, adult Christians have a biblical worldview. This has a profound effect on our ability to respond to the world around us. A biblical worldview means that we actually believe that the teachings of the Bible are truth and relevant to real life. This means that fewer than one-in-ten professing Christians over eighteen years of age believes in absolute moral values. It is no wonder that there is virtually no difference in lifestyle between the world and the church. It seems that we have succumbed to a platonic spirituality that makes an unbiblical dichotomy between the spiritual and the material.

The worldview of the majority in post-Christian America is agnostic materialism. By this I mean that most people believe God is unknowable. They believe God is a higher power that can be experienced by many different traditions and can be called upon by many different names. Most believe you cannot have a personal relationship with God. On the other hand, materialism is the ultimate goal of most people. Barna found that when asked what constitutes success in life, few Christians responded in spiritual terms. Most responded in relation to professional achievement, asset acquisition, and physical accomplishments.

We live in a live-and-let-live culture. It is a worldview that sees absolutes as intolerant and compromise as a necessary part of life. The problem is that this is also the worldview of the majority of professing believers sitting in church pews every Sunday.

This live-and-let-live attitude is a real problem because it dulls the ability for people to be critically reflective about the consequences of ignoring and denying biblical truth. The attempt to move the church as a whole through objective teaching becomes increasingly difficult. It is probably this lukewarm mentality that is spoken of in the Bible as a description of the church in the last days. See if this sounds familiar:

> And to the angel of the church in Laodicea write: The Amen, the faithful and true Witness, the Beginning of the creation of God, says this: "I know your deeds that you are neither cold nor hot; I would that you were cold or hot. So because you are lukewarm, and neither hot nor cold, I will spit you out of My mouth. Because you say, 'I am rich, and have become wealthy, and have need of nothing,' and you do not know that you are wretched and miserable and poor and blind and naked, I advise you to buy from Me gold refined by fire, that you may become rich, and white garments, that you may clothe yourself, and that the shame of your nakedness may not be revealed; and eye salve to anoint your eyes, that you may see. Those whom I love, I reprove and discipline; be zealous therefore, and repent. Behold, I stand at the door and knock; if anyone hears My voice and opens the door, I will come in to him, and will dine with him, and he with Me." Revelation 3:14-20

Notice that this warning and invitation was written to a church that was compromised in its worldview and comfortable in its lifestyle. The sad thing is that they could not even see their problem. We are living in this age. If we were honest, this description would be declared to be a very accurate portrayal of most churches today.

To overcome this dilemma requires nothing short of a change in our worldview. This is a significant problem because worldviews do not dwell in the mind but in the heart. We need to do more than change our minds. We must somehow experience a change of heart. Our worldview is based upon the assumptions we hold about reality. These assumptions develop over time from our training and our experiences in life. Once something works to solve a problem with some consistency, we then assume it to be truth. Without a worldview based upon the Truth of the Bible, we develop our own truths through training and experience. It is very hard to contradict these assumptions without developing the skills of critical thinking and objective obedience to God's Word as Truth.

If I tell you that I will give you a million dollars if you jump from an airplane with no parachute, you will probably decline the invitation because of the assumptions you have about the possibility of surviving such an event. If you met someone who was a new millionaire because he took the offer, you would be full of questions and ready to reevaluate your first opinion. When he explained that the plane was sitting on the ground, and he jumped into an airbag, you would sadly acknowledge that your assumptions had kept you from becoming a millionaire.

This is what we are facing today in the church. The lifestyle the Bible describes is so contrary to what the world assumes will work that people daily turn down God's invitation to spiritual riches and blessings. Asking people to love their grumbling spouse, antagonistic neighbor, or personal enemy makes about as much sense as jumping out of an airplane with no parachute. Telling people that giving and forgiving are the way to blessing may get an "amen" on Sunday, but most people sitting in the pew doubt that it will work in the real world they face on Monday. Our worldview is how we live – not what we profess. It reveals what is in our heart not what is in our heads. The church is so much like the world because it assumes the same things as the world.

An interesting part of the invitation God gives us as last day Christians is to come and receive "eye salve to anoint our eyes that we may see." Our worldview is very important because it affects how we see things. We do not "see, therefore we believe," but rather, "we believe, therefore we see." It was probably easier for you to read chapter four than it is for you to read this chapter. That is because we all see ourselves as people who have confidence in God, but we are also keenly aware that our lives are not innocent in regard to the lifestyle of the Scriptures. Chapters four, five, six, and seven are building blocks. It takes confidence in God and His Word in order to walk contrary to the majority worldview. It takes a life of innocence, humility, and vulnerability to express biblical love. It takes confidence, innocence, and love to bring glory to God. As a reader, you are wasting your time to move forward in this book if you are unable to critically examine your everyday lifestyle in light of the Bible and allow God to open your eyes to what He already sees.

When you and I are willing to trust God and obey His Word even though it seems like He is asking us to jump out of an airplane without a parachute, then and only then, will we be able to walk as Daniel said, innocent before God and toward men. As a result, other Christians may be willing to reevaluate their assumptions when you and I walk in a way they believe is impossible in the current culture. Who knows, maybe the world will even take notice that "they who have the Son have life and they who have not the Son have not life." (1 John 5:12)

Restoring Innocence

If the statistics we read and the behavior we observe are true, then there is a great need for repentance and restoration for most Christians. We must turn from our agnostic, materialistic worldview with its partial obedience and survival tactics. We must embrace a biblical worldview which leads us to spiritual victory that is both liberating and empowering. Consider how God sees us as it is revealed in 1 John 5:1-5:

> Whoever believes that Jesus is the Christ is born of God; and whoever loves the Father loves the child born of Him. By this we know that we love the children of God, when we love God and observe His commandments. For this is the love of God, that we keep His commandments; and His commandments are not burdensome. For whatever is born of God overcomes the world; and this is the victory that has overcome the world — our faith. And who is the one who overcomes the world, but he who believes that Jesus is the Son of God.

God's sees us as His children born into His family through His Son, Jesus Christ. He sees His children loving one another as evidence that we love Him. (Here is a starting point for many Christians.) This is not a subjective feeling but rather an objective obedience to God's commands. God's commandments are not burdensome to those who are keeping them out of love rather than religious duty. Underlying our ability to act in loving obedience is our faith, which is deeply influenced by our assumptions and our worldview.

True faith is heart-based not head-based. Christ stands at the door of our heart and knocks. When we open our heart to Him He will come in and dwell with us. That sounds easy enough but it really is very difficult.

My father once gave my mother a gift. He hired two cleaning ladies to come to our house to give it a thorough cleaning from top to bottom. Things were very hectic for my mother and she was not able to do the deep cleaning that she wanted to do. This was not a judgment on my mother but rather an attempt to help her and give her some relief. She spent the next several days slaving over the house to make it presentable and clean to the cleaning ladies. This scenario is played out in our lives when we confess that over time our once-over-lightly approach to Christian living has taken its toll. We instinctively want to clean it up before we invite someone to come in and help. We may even decide we can do it ourselves without exposing our situation.

God is not knocking on the door of our heart so He can come to inspect and condemn our life. He already sees things as they are. He is knocking to come in and enable us to live the victorious life that He desires for us as His child.

Restoring innocence begins with getting real with God and then extends to vulnerable honesty with others. The world may take away your possessions. It may take away your freedom. It may even take your life, but we should never let it take away our innocent standing before God and men. It is in this standing that we find the liberating empowerment to live a victorious Christian life.

As Jesus was crucified with thieves, a centurion who watched Him die began praising God and said, "Certainly this man was innocent." (Luke 23:46-48) Oh, that this would be the concluding summary of our lives.

Our Christian response must be framed in innocence. Consider this admonishment as we close out this chapter:

> So then, my beloved, just as you have always obeyed, not as in my presence only, but now much more in my absence, work out your salvation with fear and trembling; for it is God who is at work in

you, both to will and to work for His good pleasure. Do all things without grumbling or disputing; that you may prove yourselves to be <u>blameless</u> and <u>innocent</u>, children of God above reproach in the midst of a crooked and perverse generation, among whom you appear as lights in the world, holding fast the word of life, so that in the day of Christ I may have cause to glory because I did not run in vain nor toil in vain. Philippians 2:12-17 *Emphasis mine.*

RESPONDING WITH COMPASSION

And so, as those who have been chosen of God, holy and beloved, put on a heart of compassion , kindness, humility, gentleness and patience; bearing with one another, and forgiving each other, whoever has a complaint against anyone; just as the Lord forgave you, so also should you.

Colossians 3:12-13

CHAPTER SIX

Responding with Compassion

—ɯ—

The Hallmark of Christianity

We are now entering into terrain that is so known to the Christian that there will be a temptation to race through it. I assure you that the kind of love that marks the Christian is far above the realm of normal human love. It has been my experience that many lost people demonstrate more love than professing Christian people. The love they demonstrate is not the love that is being spoken of when we refer to the hallmark love of the Christian. At best their love is a "phileo" love that is based on kindness and emotion. The "agapeo" love that God calls the Christian to manifest is a selfless love founded in obedience and faith. The Christian is called to go beyond loving his own friends and family, loving his neighbor, or loving the unloved, all of which the world can do. He is called to love his enemy and the unlovely. This is the issue we must settle in this chapter. These are more than suggestions. They are commands! This is the hallmark that sets the true Christian apart from all other people. In fact, consider this injunction from Jesus Himself:

You have heard that it was said, "You shall love your neighbor, and hate your enemy." But I say to you, love your enemies, and pray for those who persecute you in order that you may be sons of your Father who is in heaven; for He causes His sun to rise on the evil and the good, and sends rain on the righteous and the unrighteous. For if you love those who love you, what reward have you? Do not even the tax-gatherers do the same? And if you greet your brothers only, what do you do more than others? Do not even the Gentiles do the same? Therefore you are to be perfect, as your heavenly Father is perfect. Matt 5:43-48

You might want to read that again! This is one of those portions of Scripture that almost every Christian is familiar with, but we put it in the area of supernatural and are not in the habit of practicing it. As a matter of fact, it is as though we believe that "God can't be serious." How is it possible that we can love people who persecute us or even desire to kill us? Consider also these passages:

If possible, so far as it depends on you, be at peace with all men. Never take your own revenge, beloved, but leave room for the wrath of God, for it is written, "Vengeance is Mine, I will repay," says the Lord. "But if your enemy is hungry, feed him, and if he is thirsty, give him a drink; for in so doing you will heap burning coals upon his head." Do not be overcome by evil, but overcome evil with good. Romans 12:18-21

By this the children of God and the children of the devil are obvious: anyone who does not practice righteousness is not of God, nor the one who does not love his brother. 1 John 3:10

This is the kind of love that sets Christians apart from all other human beings. This is the kind of compassion that is a fruit of the Holy Spirit. If you and I are truthful, we must admit that it is hard to hate people or hold a grudge if we are walking with the Lord.

A Biblical Definition of Love

Many years ago I had the privilege of being the commencement speaker at a Bible institute graduation of a young man who had come to Christ in my ministry in mid-coast Maine. As I considered all the difficulties these men and women would face as they entered into the ministry, God led me to 1 Corinthians 13. I have also preached it to the graduates of a Bible institute I helped establish in Haiti.

Formal training in ministry often causes us to rely on knowledge, spiritual gifts, and talent to accomplish the ministry. Before we can share our knowledge, use our spiritual gifts, or apply our talent, the people to whom we are ministering must know we love them. If we are going to effectively respond to a threatening world, it is imperative that we function in the atmosphere of love. I personally believe this passage is the greatest definition of love found anywhere. Without love we are nothing, and everything we attempt to accomplish will amount to nothing. This passage of Scripture is the gold standard by which we must gauge our lives and our ministries. It needs to become daily reading until it becomes the daily principle that rules our lives.

If I speak with the tongues of men and of angels, but do not have love, I have become a noisy gong or a clanging cymbal. And if I have the gift of prophecy, and know all mysteries and all knowledge; and if I have all faith, so as to remove mountains, but do not have love, I am nothing. And if I give all my possessions to feed the poor, and if I deliver my body to be burned, but do not have love, it profits me nothing. Love is patient, love is kind, and is not jealous; love does not brag and is not arrogant, does not act unbecomingly; it does not seek its own, is not provoked, does not take into account a wrong suffered, does not rejoice in unrighteousness, but rejoices with the truth; bears all things, believes all things, hopes all things, endures all things. 1 Corinthians 13:1-8

If 1 Corinthians 13 is the definition of love, Jesus Christ is the example of love. Studying the life of Christ and meditating on 1 Corinthians 13 will prove to be of great assistance in overcoming the loveless, pharisaical tendencies we have as religious people. Biblical love does not compromise Truth, but it yearns for others to benefit from the Truth and not be slain by it. If love is without holiness it is not biblical love, and if holiness is without love it is not biblical holiness. God is both holy and love in His essence. We should be both holy and love in our lifestyles and in our response to the world around us.

Very often when we emphasize two humanities, one lost and one saved, we appear to have an attitude of exclusiveness, prejudice, and ugliness. It is true that there are both saved and lost people, but both are made in the image of God. Some are still in rebellion against God and some, by His grace, have raised the flag of surrender and been welcomed home as prodigal sons.

We need to understand that all human beings have been made in the image of God, and all trace their origins back to common parents in Adam and Eve. When we view the lost, we are looking at our earthly brothers and sisters targeted by God's wrath, just as we once were. (Romans 1:18; 2:5-8; Ephesians 2:1-10) They will remain in this position until they yield to His redemption which is found in the subsitutionary death of His Son for mankind's sin.

Compassion is not limited to our believing brothers and sisters to the exclusion of our non-believing brothers and sisters. We are to have pity on all men just as Christ had pity on us.

Who is Our Enemy?

We do have a spiritual enemy. Satan is the spiritual enemy of all God's children. He roams about as a lion seeking whom he may devour. (1 Peter 5:8) He schemes to take advantage of us. (2 Corinthians 2:11) He hinders us. (1 Thessalonians 2:18) We do well to remember that our battle is a spiritual battle just as the Scriptures say:

> Finally, be strong in the Lord, and in the strength of His might. Put on the full armor of God, that you may be able to stand firm against the schemes of the Devil. For our struggle is not against flesh and blood, but against the rulers, against the powers, against the world forces of this darkness, against the spiritual forces of wickedness in the heavenly places. Ephesians 6:10-12

What about our flesh and blood enemies? What about the neighbor who will not keep his dog on the leash? What about the person at work who spreads hateful rumors about you? What about the liberal anti-Christian politician? What about the abortionist? What about the Muslim? Are we willing to feed him when he is hungry or give her a drink when she is thirsty? Is our confrontation with these people full of compassion with a desire to see them saved and set free?

Distinguishing the Participants in Spiritual Warfare

While I was participating as a local pastor in anti-abortion activity in Buffalo, New York, I was faced with this dilemma. We often faced pro-abortion demonstrators who were abusive and in-your-face. They were sincere in their desire to prevent Christians from exposing and interfering with abortions being performed in the Buffalo area. We were in conflict with the Buffalo police as they attempted to uphold laws that protected the abortionist who was killing unwanted children. The first rescue that I attended caused me to experience the peace and grace that comes when a Christian is involved in an earthly conflict that is the consequence of a spiritual battle.

It was a very cold February morning in Buffalo. The wind was blowing off the frozen lake, and the pro-life rescue demonstration was at a stalemate as the police stood like a wall around the Christians who were sitting in front of the abortion clinic door. This was my first experience observing an Operation Rescue event as a local pastor. My heart was broken at the thought that this was a place where hundreds of unborn children routinely lost their lives.

As the number of Christians sitting in front of the door of the abortion clinic dwindled due to arrests, I felt compelled to put myself between the unborn children and their scheduled execution at the hands of the abortionist. I knew that if the door was opened I would become a spectator as children were put to death.

My mind flashed back to a scene of people in the city watching as a victim was mugged and doing nothing about it. I knew I could not stand by without doing everything within my power as a Christian to prevent children from dying on that day.

As I crawled on my hands and knees up to the line of police officers who were preventing new people from getting to the door, I prayed for courage and wisdom. The sound of hands being rubbed together in an attempt to keep warm caused me to look up at a female officer who was dutifully standing guard. For the first time I saw her as an unwilling participant in this spiritual drama that was playing itself out on Elmwood Street. I felt compelled to offer her my warm thermal gloves and did so. After first declining the offer, she finally took the gloves. Probing down the line, I was finally permitted to move to the door by an officer who was apparently sympathetic to what we were attempting to do. Eventually I was arrested and taken to a local school where about one hundred other protestors were to be arraigned.

Meanwhile my wife was notified of my arrest, and she and my two young sons began to pray. My son prayed that the Lord would allow me to be home in time for dinner. At the school we were informed that we would be arraigned in the order in which we were arrested. It was now about five o'clock in the evening, and I was nearly the last one arrested. I took out my New Testament and settled in for a long wait.

An officer called out the first name, James Evans. I looked around to see who the other James Evans was. My name was called a second time, and I reported to the desk. The officer to whom I had given my gloves greeted me, processed me, and gave my gloves back with a thank you. My son's prayer was answered, and I was home in time for dinner. The Lord also helped me understand how to respect the human partici-pants in a spiritual battle.

Later that year as I served as director of Project Rescue in Buffalo, I had another lesson from the Lord. Pastor Ted Cadwalder and I were the first two pastors to serve time in jail as the rescues continued to draw attention to child killing in Buffalo. The enemy had found a lightning rod to focus on. It seemed that I was continually receiving verbal assaults and was the subject of more lies and attacks.

One of the more aggressive battle fronts was in Amherst, a suburb of Buffalo. As I was walking across the parking lot behind the strip plaza where the abortion clinic was located, I encountered the abortionist going to his car. We both froze in a moment of awkwardness. I asked him if I could have a word with him. He hesitantly agreed, and after exchanging courteous formalities I asked him if he would be interested in reading a book written by a former abortionist who at one time ran the largest abortion clinic in America. Sharing with him that this man stopped performing abortions for medical reasons, I offered to bring him a copy. The book, <u>Aborting America</u>, was written by Dr. Bernard Nathanson. He said he would like to read the book, so I told him I would return with a copy for him.

That afternoon, as I entered the front door of the abortion clinic and asked for the abortionist, the staff went crazy. When the doctor came out to greet me, I suggested we go outside where we talked, and I gave him the book along with a gospel tract to use as a bookmark. The Lord had given me the grace to see this enemy in the battle of abortion as a lost, blind human who was in the bondage of sin.

I share these stories with you to try to help you understand that it is imperative that we distinguish between the participants in the spiritual warfare. We must show respect to authorities and concern for the lost. In the flesh this is impossible, but in the Lord it becomes a compelling desire. As I said before, these are building blocks. Without a foundation of confidence in God and His Word and a life of innocence before God and man, it will be impossible to manifest the love that I am talking about. This is what lies at the heart of compassionate confrontation.

The Sin and the Sinner Syndrome

We have all been exposed to the "hate the sin and love the sinner" cliché that is a part of our Christian rhetoric. Truth be known, most people have a hard time separating the sin from the sinner. I say this because of the hateful things I have heard Christians say about homosexuals, drug addicts, and liberal politicians. I sometimes catch myself failing to keep the two separate, but we all have to look beyond the behavior and see the sin-blinded person. God looked beyond our behavior, and while we were His enemies he died for our sins to give us eternal life. (Romans 5:8) We must make this more than a cliché and make it a reputed characteristic of a true Christian.

The year was 1990. While establishing a campaign against the liberal, democratic incumbent of the 124th New York State Assembly District, I held a press conference to make a statement concerning the recent newspaper article that announced that student funds at the State University of New York (SUNY) Binghamton would be used to sponsor a homosexual club on campus. Three local pastors were invited to stand with me at the conference. We had a good representation of the local media as well as three young men from the SUNY campus who said they were reporters for the campus newspaper.

After the press conference ended, the three SUNY students stayed behind. I took the occasion to talk to them. When asked if they were homosexuals, I heard an audible gasp from one of the three pastors that were with me. The discomfort level for my fellow pastors seemed to increase when all three young men said yes. I wanted these men to understand what I was saying in my press release. My purpose was to oppose the use of university funding to advance the sinful practice of sodomy.

Sharing my testimony with them, I assured them that I knew something about the bondage of sin. I asked them if I could pray with them and explained that I wanted to pray that God would open their eyes to their sin and set them free. One of them said, "I don't care." And the other two shrugged their shoulders. Assuming this was about as much permission as I would get considering the circumstances, I began the prayer. As I closed, a faint amen came from their direction. We shook hands, and they were assured that my door was always open to them.

When I turned around, one of the pastors who had come to attend the press conference was in tears as he said, "This is what the church should be all about." Again, I share this story to tell you the Lord has shown me that His grace is available to allow us to love those who hate us and to pray for those who despitefully use us.

These guys were not the enemy. They were brainwashed prisoners of war held in bondage in a POW camp like the one from which the Lord rescued me. They were sheep without a shepherd, the ones forgiven by martyrs as those "who know not what they do," and the reason for Christ's death. They are without hope and without God and part of the groaning creation that is separated from its creator.

When you see the homeless person with his or her sign, what do you see? When you are in line at the store, how do you view the people around you? Joni Erickson, a Christian quadriplegic and author, tells about a time when the batteries in her wheel chair ran down in the middle of the mall at Christmas time. Her husband was unavailable to call, and her shopping companion was going to be away for about another hour. At first frustration and anxiety set in as her shopping plans slipped away. Then she began to listen to the Christmas music in the mall for the first time. She began to look at all the people and families, each involved in their personal world. Eventually she began praying for the families that seemed frazzled and discouraged or the older person struggling to enjoy the day.

What was at first a major problem and inconvenience now became an opportunity to pause and look at people the way the Lord sees them. When her friend finally found her, she was somewhat disappointed to have to leave this place of quiet communion with the Lord as they together were moved with compassion for struggling people. Whenever you and I are in communion with the Lord, we will have compassion on all people.

The encouragement to hate the sin but love the sinner is great, but it must be more than a cliché. Sin is the enemy of mankind. It is destroying the lives of millions of people. Jesus did not come to invite good people to attend church, He came to seek and to save that which was lost. (Luke 19:19)

Chuck Colson in his book, <u>How Now Shall We Live</u>, tells the story of Ron Greer, "an ex-offender who once hated white people." After his conversion to Christ, he became an instructor in Prison Fellowship and upon his release, a pastor at an evangelical church in Madison, Wisconsin. After distributing Christian tracts describing homosexuality as a sin, his church service was disrupted by homosexual activists who threw condoms at the pulpit and shouted obscenities. Ron Greer responded by inviting them to join in the worship service.

Later, the press asked how he kept his cool. He said, "I have no more reason to be angry with them than I would with a blind person who stepped on my foot."

The Essence of Our Response

Compassion must be the essence of our response. Compassion comes from the Hebrew "racham" which means to love, to pity, or to be merciful. Jesus was moved with compassion when he saw the multitudes because He saw them as lost sheep with no shepherd. (Matthew 9:36) I am of the persuasion that if compassion fails to move us then we should not move. Stay put until you can see the situation the way the Lord sees it. Take time to commune with God, and ask Him to give you eyes that see as He sees.

We are quick to respond in order to win the battle, gain the spotlight, or voice our opinion. Remembering that the battle has been won, Christ deserves the spotlight, and our opinion does not really count will help us keep things in perspective and temper our response. When Christ responded to us while we were yet sinners, He sacrificially responded out of love for us with a desire for our benefit. (John 3:16) May our compassionate response model that of our Lord and Savior.

FOCUSED ON GOD'S GLORY

For all things are for your sakes,
that the grace which is spreading
to more and more people may cause
the giving of thanks to abound
to the glory of God .

2 Corinthians 4:15

CHAPTER SEVEN
Focused on God's Glory

—ɷ—

The Purpose of all things

Where there is controversy there is a spotlight. A spotlight is a good thing. It draws the focus of the audience to something important. As the play goes on, the audience's eyes are looking at all the individual parts that make up the whole. There are times when a spotlight almost forces our attention to a specific person. Such is life; people busy themselves looking at things that, for some reason, attract their attention. Every once in a while the director feels it is important to highlight something he feels is important in helping people understand the his plans. So he puts a spotlight on an event or a leading character who is scripted to fill this role in revealing the director's purpose or message.

There is something about light that draws people's attention. It can be a flash of light that gets a "What was that?" response or a beam of light that causes people to say, "What's going on over there?" At times throughout life, the spotlight falls on each of us. It may be when something good happens, or it may be when something bad happens. It may involve something very personal like the loss of a loved one, or it may be very public like a controversy at work. God has designed His historic drama in such a way that he uses everyone in the cast to highlight the purpose of the play.

There are two major challenges to human beings concerning the spotlight. Some people have been afflicted with "spotlight-itis." This is a mental condition whereby the individual feels it necessary to always be in the spotlight. The condition usually develops when a person has been in the spotlight for a significant amount of time. When the spotlight is removed the individual senses a loss of identity and significance. Symptoms of this condition include running to and fro trying to stir up controversy, making outlandish public comments, seeking out people in the spotlight to try to share it with them, and ultimately, if left untreated, the patient will self-destruct in a futile attempt to satisfy his or her need for attention.

Another challenge the spotlight poses for most human beings is the challenge to "stay with the script." This problem occurs mostly when the character is unprepared. The spotlight comes on, and there is an initial panic followed by a clumsy ad lib that often distracts the audience from the purpose of the director. Many times the person is self conscious and gets out of character under pressure. On other occasions the individual second guesses the script and ad libs to try and improve it.

The spotlight is a very important tool used by the Director to accomplish His purposes. Most of the Scriptures are descriptions of scenes "under the spotlight." It behooves us to learn how God's servants respond when He spotlights them in order to reveal His purposes and the nuances of His plans. As life becomes increasingly confusing and hard to follow, the importance of following God's script increases exponentially.

Our Christian response to a threatening world must always be focused on God's glory. When the spotlight comes on us, whether it is at work or home, in private or in public, we need to stick to God's script and focus on His purposes. How can we be prepared to respond properly if we are not confidently founded in God, innocent before Him, filled with His compassion, and prepared to bring Him glory by yielding to His script for our lives?

Trophies Syndrome

If we fail to understand that it is all about Him, then we will tend to measure our lives by things that will pass away. We will attempt to find significance outside of our relationship with God. Our worth will be measured by what we perceive to be our successes, a condition known as "trophy syndrome." This chapter is beginning to sound like a medical journal, but there are certain things that have such unique symptoms that they deserve a name. It seems we are bombarded with all the new syndromes the world is using to classify unique behaviors that plague a significant group of people. Why not add a couple of our own?

Trophy syndrome is classified as the pre-occupation of an individual with his or her personal successes. If our life is measured by our personal success rather than God's glory, then we are bound to succumb to this syndrome to some degree. Trophies are remembrances of times when people acknowledged the patient's talents, brilliance, or success. These trophies range in size from family trophies, which are very small and rather commonplace, to national trophies, which are much rarer and are usually so large that they are hard to elevate over the head when they are awarded. People who are stricken with this syndrome spend hours pondering their personal trophy case. This condition is often detectible by the amount of time the patient spends talking about the trophy experiences.

Trophies are physical objects that are part of the physical world which will pass away. I had my appreciation for trophies put in perspective when we rented an old farm house that belonged to a camp in upstate New York. The barn became a storage/dumping place for everything the camp was not using. My children became quite excited when they found cases of shiny, gold, plastic trophies in the barn. There is something special about a trophy, but there is also something weird about finding cases of them in a dirty old dilapidated barn. They suddenly lose their value. Whenever I see a trophy today I cannot help but flash back to a whole barn full of trophies made by man to acknowledge man.

Paul had an eye for trophies. He told Timothy that at the end of his life he was looking forward to being awarded trophies made by God, personally for him and for all those who are excited about God's appearing. (2 Timothy 4:7,8) Earlier he listed all his earthly trophies and said they were nothing compared to the trophy he was pursuing. Consider Paul's outlook on earthly trophies. I have included some comments.

Finally, my brethren, rejoice in the Lord. To write the same things again is no trouble to me, and it is a safeguard for you. *(Note: This is like an inoculation against trophy syndrome.)* Beware of the dogs, beware of the evil workers, beware of the false circumcision; for we are the true circumcision, who worship in the Spirit of God and glory in Christ Jesus and put no confidence in the flesh, although I myself might have confidence even in the flesh. *(Note: One of the ways we succumb to this syndrome is to pay more than passing attention to those who are terminally ill with the disease; i.e., the dogs and evil workers.)* If anyone else has a mind to put confidence in the flesh, I far more: circumcised the eighth day, of the nation of Israel, of the tribe of Benjamin, a Hebrew of Hebrews; as to the Law, a Pharisee; as to zeal, a persecutor of the church; as to the righteousness which is in the Law, found blameless. But whatever things were gain to me, those things I have counted as loss for the sake of Christ. More than that, I count all things to be loss in view of the surpassing value of knowing Christ Jesus my Lord, for whom I have suffered the loss of all things, and count them but rubbish *(Note: Sounds like he is describing a pile of stuff in an old barn that was eventually burned to improve the look of the property.)* in order that I may gain Christ, and may be found in Him, not having a righteousness of my own derived from the Law, but that which is through faith in Christ, the righteousness which comes from God on the basis of faith, that I may know Him, and the power of His resurrection and the fellowship of His sufferings, being conformed to His death; in order that I may attain to the resurrection from the dead. Philippians 3:1-11

Consider Paul's way of handling the trophy syndrome. He consciously refused to keep a trophy case of all his accomplishments. If anyone had the opportunity to have a large collection of trophies, it was the apostle Paul. Instead he tossed them in the trash as he received them and moved on to seek to know more of Christ. He was Christ-indulged not self-indulged. This is the only antidote to trophy syndrome.

Tombstone Syndrome

Generally patients who are afflicted with trophy syndrome are also infected with its companion, tombstone syndrome. Tombstones are remembrances of times when people put the patient down, questioned their motives, and judged them as a failure. These tombstones fall into two categories. There are personal tombstones that are kept in a mausoleum for private viewing only, and public tombstones which the whole world can see. This condition is often detectible by the patient's continual need for reassurance.

Tombstone syndrome can be just as crippling as trophy syndrome. With this syndrome a person is pre-occupied with his failures or situations that others have declared as failures. This syndrome may be more difficult to treat than trophy syndrome because the situations that aggravate the condition are more prevalent. The condition can be aggravated by negative comments from a spouse, friends, enemies, and ultimately from Satan himself who is the accuser of the brethren.

It could be classified as a form of battle fatigue that comes as a result of losing perspective during prolonged combat. It has been witnessed throughout history in otherwise healthy people such as the prophet Elijah, and even young Timothy, who appeared to have a touch of tombstone syndrome brought on by those who challenged his leadership because of his youth.

Elijah challenged the false prophets of his day and showcased God's glory, but when Jezebel put a contract out on his life, he went and sat down under a juniper tree and said, "It is enough; now, O LORD, take my life, for I am not better than my fathers." 1 Kings 19:4-5 God's prescription for His prophet included some rest, nourishment, and a new assignment. Paul's advice to Timothy was:

> I solemnly charge you in the presence of God and of Christ Jesus and of His chosen angels, to maintain these principles without bias, doing nothing in a spirit of partiality. Do not lay hands upon anyone too hastily and thus share responsibility for the sins of others; keep yourself free from sin. No longer drink water exclusively, but use a little wine for the sake of your stomach and your frequent ailments. 1 Timothy 5:21-23

Paul gave Timothy spiritual encouragement to stay on course with his assignment from the Lord. He reminded him not to make the battle personal by showing partiality toward people but to maintain an innocent lifestyle. He also addressed his physical needs.

This syndrome is more than spiritual or mental. Our bodies are designed to be recreated through rest and good nutrition. Many of God's servants feel it is a sign of strength to push their body to its limit, when in fact, it is abusive to the vessel of which God has made them stewards. Jesus had to go aside and rest during his ministry, and He did so without apology or guilt.

We live in a world that has declared that it is involved in a rat race. The reality is that the winner will still be a rat. It would be better not to qualify for the race than to sacrifice everything of eternal importance in order to be declared the best rat on earth. I am not speaking about a life of laziness and leisure. Rather, I am talking about acknowledging that, although the battle is not against flesh and blood but against spiritual powers in heavenly places, we still do battle in a flesh and blood body that requires proper maintenance.

What about our failures? Some say we should learn from them. Some say they should be expected. I would suggest we need to be careful when we classify something as a failure. Remember, it is God who is at work to accomplish His purposes. Sometimes He uses what appear to be defeats in order to accomplish His ultimate will.

Contagious Agendas

Agendas are organized plans motivated by a specific purpose. They are contagious because they are purposeful, organized, and usually have momentum, mottos, and heroes. People can get caught up in them very easily.

For instance, the "take back the culture" agenda is a great motivator and certainly can reach beyond the limited influence of the true Christian to include patriots of all sorts. Christianity had significant influence on the culture and its founding concepts and documents, but the concept of owning a culture is erroneous at its core.

Culture, by its nature, is the sum of the core values and assumptions held by a group of people. It would appear that some who carry this banner believe that the culture will change if the right party is in control or the right people get elected. There is a tendency to believe that if the right laws are passed or blocked, we have accomplished something for the Kingdom.

Now please do not misunderstand me. I have personally participated in the political system and also believe good citizens should vote for those who best represent biblical principles. But being a co-belligerent with those who oppose legalizing sodomy, abortion, pornography, and other sinful behavior does not mean that we are allies in the purposes of God.

We are not called to "take back the culture" but rather to proclaim Truth within the culture. Some of you are cheering because you have always opposed those who got involved in politics or caught up in issues. You know we are salt, but you prefer to be a saltlick (a block of salt placed in a field to attract or feed animals) and invite people to church rather than be a salt shaker that applies salt to the culture around it. Before you consider me to be in your camp, let me say that an equally unbiblical position is one that says we are not called to address the public issues of our day.

Both these agendas take different paths to the same destination. The take-back-the-culture trail includes anxiety, frustration, power plays, and ultimately compromise in order to get the largest block of influence. The stay-out-of-issues trail includes comfort-zone church-ianity, apathy, intimidation, and ultimately compromise to avoid controversy.

We are called to confidently stand on God's Truth in such a way that He is glorified. Since culture is an atmosphere that reflects the assumptions of the heart, God is the One who changes it. He merely asks us to recognize Him in all the circumstances of life and to be conscious of His presence at all times as He touches the hearts of men. We are called to carry the Truth (preach the Gospel) into the culture (to every creature) which also means taking the Truth into the public debate over the issues of life.

Mother's Cake

What we are discussing is difficult. It will create hardships and relationships that are very uncomfortable and are sometimes hard to swallow.

We can all quote Romans 8:28 which says that all things are working together for good to those who love the Lord and are called according to His purpose. It is a verse that is easy to quote but often hard to believe. I love chocolate cake and especially a chocolate cake that my wife makes from a recipe given to her by her friend, Nancy Callister. The recipe actually goes back to Nancy's mother and has been given the name "Mother's Cake." The ingredients include:

2 cups of flour
2 cups of sugar
2 teaspoons of baking soda
1 teaspoon of baking powder
½ teaspoon of salt
¾ cup of cocoa
2 eggs
½ cup of oil
1 cup of hot coffee
1 cup of milk

Mix together and bake at 350 degrees for ½ hour.

Now we will take the Romans 8:28 view of this cake. For breakfast you will be served two cups of flour. For lunch you must eat two cups of sugar and two teaspoons of baking soda. As an evening snack you will be served one teaspoon of baking powder, half a teaspoon of salt, and three quarters of a cup of powdered cocoa. Tomorrow you will be forced to eat two raw eggs chased down with half a cup of cooking oil. For lunch you will be served a cup of hot coffee. (That will seem like a great meal compared to the rest.) For dinner, at the end of the final day, you may have a refreshing cup of milk.

Ingredient by ingredient this cake would be hard to take. Each meal would have its challenges and blessings. Some things are hard to swallow. Other things are hard to understand. Some days go just fine (coffee and milk days). However, when all the ingredients are put together and baked, a miracle takes place that transforms them into a delicious cake.

This is true of life also. All things (all the ingredients of life) are working out for good (have a place in the recipe) to all those who love God and are called according to His purposes. Some of the ingredients in life are hard to swallow, but I have to remind myself that God is the Chef and that He is making a cake in my life that I will proclaim as good.

Consider Joseph, who believed God was going to accomplish something in his life. He was hated by his brothers, sold into slavery in Egypt, and thrown in jail on false charges. He was a real man, and I am sure he felt real pain when his brothers and even his father mocked him. He must have felt humiliation and failure when he was sold into slavery. He must have felt anger and fear when he was falsely accused of infidelity and imprisoned. His life looked like a field of tombstones.

However, as far as we can see, he continued to believe God and maintained his integrity and work ethic in all the situations in which he found himself. God used all these things to put Joseph on his mark on the stage, so that when the spotlight turned to him he could proclaim the glory of God.

When Joseph's brothers came before him to beg for food to relieve the toll the famine had taken on their family, all the angels in heaven waited to hear Joseph's response. Joseph's brothers were also concerned about how the brother they had so badly abused would treat them. Here is the account with some comments inserted.

When Joseph's brothers saw that their father was dead, they said, "What if Joseph should bear a grudge against us and pay us back in full for all the wrong which we did to him!" *(Note: People generally know what they deserve and what to expect. These guys were basically saying, "What if Joseph responds the way we would respond?")* So they sent a message to Joseph, saying, "Your father charged before he died, saying, 'Thus you shall say to Joseph, Please forgive, I beg you, the transgression of your brothers and their sin, for they did you wrong.' And now, please forgive the transgression of the servants of the God of your father." And Joseph wept when they spoke to him. (Note: *After all he had been through, Joseph still remained tender and compassionate.*) Then his brothers also came and fell down before him and said, "Behold, we are your servants." But Joseph said to them, "Do not be afraid, for am I in God's place. *(Note: Joseph never lost sight of God's presence and work in his life.)* And as for you, you meant evil against me, but God meant it for good in order to bring about this present result, to preserve many people alive. So therefore, do not be afraid; I will provide for you and your little ones." So he comforted them and spoke kindly to them. Genesis 50:15-21

Joseph's response was basically, "Hey, God is at work here, and His work is always good." Joseph surely did not enjoy every ingredient God had brought into his life, but he trusted God and desired to bring Him glory. He had confidence in God, was innocent before God and toward man, was compassionate, and gave God the glory. When the spotlight came on, and the entire audience's attention was focused on this scene, Joseph used the occasion to glorify God.

Spotlight-itis, trophy and tombstone syndromes, and contagious agendas are afflictions that affect us when our spiritual immune system is weakened and the opportunistic viruses of the flesh infect our thinking. The best way to avoid these conditions is to feed on God's Word, take care of your physical body, trust God, maintain an innocent lifestyle, love people, and focus on God's glory.

Asking the Right Question

I am fascinated by the game of golf and attempt to play when time and finances permit. I have taken some group lessons, read many magazine articles, and spend most of my television viewing time watching the golf channel. It is interesting to me that there are contradicting theories concerning club grip, addressing the ball, movement of the knees, hips, shoulders, elbows, and hands. (About the only thing that everyone agrees on is that one's head should remain still.) On a golf club commercial I saw a robot hit perfect shots with no knees, hips, elbows, hands, or even a head. I have come to realize that all that really matters is that the club face hits the ball properly. Everything else is an attempt to make that situation happen more consistently.

I have learned that when I try to dissect my golf swing into all the little components, I get so focused on those things that I tense up and play even worse. The problem with this kind of thinking is that it actually distracts me from the purpose of all the contortions and alignments. The purpose is to make the club face come in contact with the ball properly. The club is capable of a perfect game; it is the golfer that is the problem.

The same thing is true about our Christian walk. There appears to be a lot involved in responding correctly. Do I have enough confidence in God's Word? How innocent can an imperfect person be? How can I control my human reaction when faced with enemies?

It is possible to have a proper Christian response in a post-Christian world. Jesus demonstrated this to us when He walked on earth. We have to be careful that we avoid getting hung up on all the parts and miss out on the purpose of the parts. What really matters is that God receives the glory. Everything else is an attempt to make that happen more frequently and with better results.

I still read golf magazine articles, and I watch other golfers who seem to have some degree of success in the game. But I have now shifted my confidence from <u>my</u> ability to hit a good shot to the <u>club's</u> ability to hit a perfect shot. My goal is to allow the club to do what it was designed to do.

The same is true of our Christian walk. We can not have confidence in <u>our</u> ability but rather in <u>God's</u> ability to work in our lives.

As I close this chapter I want to encourage you to focus on one simple question that will help you in your adjustment of the other elements we have looked at so far in this book. Here is the controlling question in all that we do:

"How can God be glorified in this moment, circumstance, or situation?"

RESPONDING RADICALLY

*"I call for Christian radicals,
and especially young Christian radicals,
to stand up in loving confrontation,
but confrontation — looking to the living Christ
moment by moment for strength —
in loving confrontation
with all that is wrong and destructive
in the church, our culture, and the state."*

Francis A. Schaeffer
The Great Evangelical Disaster

CHAPTER EIGHT

Responding Radically

—ᴍ—

What is a Radical?

What imagery comes to mind when you hear the word radical? Recently we have become accustomed to the word radical in describing terrorists. It is important that we understand what Francis Schaeffer was looking for when he called for a generation of Christian radicals.

Webster's Dictionary lists three aspects of the word radical:

1: of, relating to, or proceeding from a root 2: of or relating to the origin 3: tending or disposed to make extreme changes in existing views, habits, conditions, or institutions

It is interesting that the third aspect of radical is the most common understanding. However, the first two are closer to the foundational meaning — proceeding from a root or relating to the origin.

All things are in the process of change. This is the nature of life. But the things of God never change. They have a life of their own. Have you ever tried to remove bamboo from your yard? If there is even one inch of root left in the ground, the bamboo will come back and once again attempt to take over the yard. It is a radical plant! If you are tired of bamboo and you want to remove it, you will have a difficult time.

The same is true of God's presence in the world. He is the Origin. He is the Root and Stem of Jesse that springs forth with fruit. When God continues to be present in a world that rejects Him, His followers will be counted as radical. This is a word that people use to intimidate and malign, and yet it is the same description given to the disciples when they were called "the ones who are turning the world upside down." They were in fact turning the world right-side up. What I am calling for in this book is nothing short of radical Christian living. This means Christian living that is as close to the original desire of God as is possible.

What we need is a generation of Christians who are springing forth from the Root, full of sap, bearing fruit to the glory of God. There are several things standing in the way of the church as a whole that will be addressed in this chapter. Those Christians who attempt to abide in the Vine and draw strength from the Root will be seen as those disposed to making extreme changes in views, habits, and traditions.

It would appear that post-Christian America has cleared out the troublesome bamboo of God's presence from its landscape, but a closer look will reveal fresh shoots emerging from the soil. God is touching the hearts of thousands of His people who can no longer find pleasure in being restrained by compromised lives that are void of true compassion and useless to the Kingdom of God.

Let me be clear here. I am not calling for a generation of rebels. Webster defines a rebel as someone who opposes or takes up arms against a country or ruler, someone who is disobedient or rebellious. There is a tendency to become rebellious in troublesome times, but we are called to submission; first to God, then to those in authority (parents, spouse, elders, government officials), and even to our circumstances, realizing that God works through each of these to accomplish His will and to glorify His name.

What is a radical? A radical is someone who believes that God is still in control, and His Word is still relevant to all issues of life and faith. He has confidence in God. He is innocent before God and man. He is moved with compassion and sees the glory of God as his ultimate aim.

Truth and Error

Is ultimate reality God or Cosmos? Is there a supernatural reality, or is what we see all that exists? Is there absolute truth, or is everything relative, situational, and personal? Do our lives have purpose, or are we merely the result of nature with no meaning other than existence? How we answer these questions will determine how we respond to the issues and situations of life.

Post-Christian America is a reality, and there is an increasing intolerance of Christian doctrine. The civil authorities seem to be at odds with us, but are we to be at odds with them? Eight-year-old Luke Mancari summed it up when he looked out the window of his family car and saw a car load of teenagers carrying on in a reckless way. Quietly, to himself and yet overheard by an aunt that sat next to him, he said, "We live in a wicked world." As you and I ponder the world around us, how will we respond?

One of the problems we face as Christians in twenty-first century America is that the concept of absolutes is non-existent, not only outside the church but sadly within the organized church as well. Situational ethics and moral anarchy are no longer considered wrong but normal and possibly in vogue. Christians have been trained to bite their tongues in public, and as a result have a tendency to wag their tongues in private and in the security of Christian gatherings. This has profound consequences. First, it withholds needed Truth from people who are literally dying in error. Secondly, it encourages backbiting, gossip, and unfruitful negativity within the church. Finally, it gives credence to the charge of hypocrisy that is leveled against the church.

Truth has an antithesis. This means that two opposing viewpoints can both be wrong, but they can not both be right. Everyone knows this. We believe that if we pick and choose which truth will be less offensive, we can recruit more people and avoid being called troublemakers. Troublemakers are not always bad people. Remember when Ahab saw Elijah he said "Is this you, you troubler of Israel? Elijah replied, "I have not troubled Israel, but you and your father's house have, because you have forsaken the commandments of the Lord and you have followed the Baals." (1Kings 18:17,18)

Martin Luther was asked to stop being a troublemaker when he began to publicly proclaim justification by faith not works. If he would just back off this dogma which cut to the heart of the Roman brand of Christianity that controlled the people with a doctrine of works and indulgences, he would be left alone. Listen to his response:

> If I profess with the loudest voice and clearest exposition every portion of the truth of God <u>except precisely that little point which the world and the devil are at that moment attacking,</u> I am not confessing Christ, however boldly I may be professing Christ. Where the battle rages, there the loyalty of the soldier is proved; and to be steady on all the battlefield besides, is mere flight and disgrace if he flinches at that point. Martin Luther (worldofquotes.com) *Emphasis mine.*

If divorce is wrong, then it cannot also be right. It should be avoided at all costs, and when it does happen it should be mourned as a sad and tragic event. It should be preached as sin in our pulpits. It should be disciplined as sin in our churches, and it should be taught as sin to our children. This is not a hard stand, it is a Biblical standard.

Homosexuality is sin. The practice of homosexuality should be preached as sin and disciplined as sin. Abortion is a murderous sin. It should be preached as sin and disciplined as sin. Fornication, adultery, and pornography are all sins. They must be preached as sin and disciplined as sin. We are often guilty of picking and choosing which of these we will call sin, who we will hold accountable, and when that particular sin is acceptable because of the particular circumstances.

We have lost all our credibility before a watching world and the next generation. We profess to be Bible believers who believe God's Word is Truth but live lives that are at best compromised and possibly in total denial of the lifestyle spoken of in the Scriptures.

Theology of Prosperity

America has a theology of prosperity, but it has no theology of persecution. It advocates a faith without risks and a salvation that buys a better life. This paradigm is contrary to all the teachings of Scripture and all the testimony of true saints of God. Consider these passages. I have included some comments:

These things I have spoken to you, that in Me you may have peace. In the world you have tribulation, but take courage; I have overcome the world. John 16:33

Do not marvel, brethren, if the world hates you. 1 John 3:13

Blessed are you when men hate you, and ostracize you, and cast insults at you, and spurn your name as evil, for the sake of the Son of Man. (*Note: This is one of the only blessings of God that we try to avoid, or is it that we do not believe it?*) Be glad in that day, and leap for joy, for behold, your reward is great in heaven; for in the same way their fathers used to treat the prophets. But woe to you who are rich, for you are receiving your comfort in full. Woe to you who are well-fed now, for you shall be hungry. Woe to you who laugh now, for you shall mourn and weep. Woe to you when all men speak well of you, for in the same way their fathers used to treat the false prophets. (*Note: False prophets are those who tell people what they want to hear rather than what they need to hear. They tickle people's ears but never step on their toes.*) Luke 6:22-26

These are only a few of the many Scriptures that remind us that the world is no friend of God or His children. They remind us that our reward is not found in the comforts and security of this world but rather in the rewards and blessing that are to come. We must search the Scriptures and develop a biblical theology of persecution if we are ever going to risk the comforts of our prosperity. If we fail to step forward, we will also never understand the grace of God that is available to those who choose to live a God pleasing life in a post-Christian nation.

Camps and Confusion

Along with the erroneous theology of prosperity, we perpetuate an equally unbiblical and devastating theology of sectarianism. If we are ever going to see God glorified through His Church, then we must see an end to camp labels and feuds in the family of God. This is not to say that we should compromise core doctrine for the sake of unity. It means that we have to understand there is one God, one

Savior, one Gospel, and one true universal, invisible Church. The true church is found in its visible form as a massive field of wheat and tares consisting of many ecclesiastical traditions. There are different ways to express worship, different debates over manuscripts and versions of the Bible, different beliefs about church government, eschatology, spiritual gifts, dress, music, etc.

The real issue is: Man is born as a fallen soul without a hope of heaven. God gave His Son to pay for the sin of fallen man. Jesus Christ arose from the dead to verify His role as the Redeemer of fallen man. Salvation comes when man confesses his sinful condition and turns to Jesus Christ for forgiveness and life, at which time he is born again by the Holy Spirit. This is the Gospel to lost mankind. Much of the rest will be under debate until the Lord comes.

It is understandable that people who believe a certain way about other issues of faith would come together in a corporate manner as seen in a local church. But it is not acceptable for them to be unloving, uncooperative, and unkind to brethren of like faith who differ in non-essentials.

Camps and the confusion they create are nothing short of signs of carnality and immaturity. Lest I be considered some ecumenical heretic or am accused of championing some personal issue, I will let the Scriptures speak to the subject.

> And I, brethren, could not speak to you as to spiritual men, but as to men of flesh, as to babes in Christ. I gave you milk to drink, not solid food; for you were not yet able to receive it. Indeed, even now you are not yet able, for you are still fleshly. For since there is jealousy and strife among you, are you not fleshly, and are you not walking like mere men? For when one says, "I am of Paul," and another, "I am of Apollos," are you not mere men? What then is Apollos? And what is Paul? 1 Corinthians 3:1-5

We are walking as mere men today. We boast of our church as being the best in the county. Our denomination is doing its exclusive work in missions. Some camps only support their own missionaries. (But they do not restrict their own from getting support from others.) We market ourselves, criticize, and compete with other churches as though we were building our own little enterprises rather than serving the living God.

Camps and confusion must end if we are going to allow the world to see the witness of a resurrected Christ. We are called to love the brethren and lay down our lives for them. This is how the world is to know that we are Christians.

I have many Christian friends who hold different doctrines in non-essential areas. We disagree, but we are not disagreeable. I believe there is a correct interpretation of Scripture. Two opposing views may both be wrong, but they can not both be right. I want to know what is right, so I listen to opposing views and continually search out the Scriptures.

One of the drawbacks of not associating with camps that have differing views on non-essential things is that we are not driven to the Scriptures, and we remain confident in our own traditions. A tradition is a preference that becomes an assumption that it is no longer questioned. Some believe that even the Scriptures must yield to a tradition. "I know that's not what the Bible says but we . . ."

The disciples were accused of transgressing the traditions of the day. Today they might be charged with standing on the platform in church with no coat and tie, or using the wrong version of the Bible, or raising their hands during a worship service. Jesus asked the Pharisees why they transgressed the commandments of God for sake of their traditions. You see, our traditions often take the same profound significance. We run around judging others who do not walk by our traditions, while we stumble at walking in accordance with the Scriptures that say, love your brother. They even warn that the absence of love for the brethren may be a revelation of an unregenerate religious condition. (1 John 3:13-16)

If we can not have honest debate in the church family, how can we expect to engage a lost culture in debate?

Compassionate Confrontation

Compassionate confrontation is a principle that has been a guide for me since first encountering it in the early 1980's in the writings of Francis Schaeffer. Truth demands confrontation. When you tell someone they are going the wrong way or doing the wrong thing, there is going to be confrontation. If you tell them because you want to help them, and you are truly concerned for them and are willing to continue to love them even if they refuse your warning, then you are practicing compassionate confrontation.

Many years ago I was engaged in my annual confrontation of homosexuality at the state capitol of Maine. Each year, gay rights legislation would be sponsored, and each year I would go to the capitol to give testimony against it. During that season there would also be local demonstrations and confrontations.

While I was at the capitol, I saw a young lady was a member of the lesbian club at the University of Maine. She and I had spoken at one of the local demonstrations in Belfast, Maine. We met in the hallway outside the committee meeting room and she said, "Pastor Evans, you are a nice guy. Why do you keep saying such hurtful things about my lifestyle?" I told her, "When we met before, I tried to tell you that your house was on fire, but you refused to listen. I could walk away and let you burn, but if I really love you I have to continue to tell you and hope that you will flee your sin and discover the life God intended for you to live in His Son." Several of her friends saw us talking and called for her to come with them. She responded, "Go ahead, I'll come later. I want to talk with Pastor Evans." I have been amazed at how many people are willing to discuss very sensitive issues once they find out you are not out to hurt them.

To be accommodating and tolerant may sound Christian, but it is not. We can not ignore or change Scriptures to accommodate the world. We are bound to proclaim and live by the Scriptures and the Scriptures alone.

We cannot preach and live only in the areas of Christianity that do not bother the world. We cannot pick and choose which issues we will consider serious.

We do not confront to win the battle, for the battle has already been won. We do not confront to hurt or put down the person, for this is a person for whom Christ died. We share the Truth with our toes curled up in our shoes and a lump in our throat. We share the Truth in love and yet in its pure, undiluted form. We share the Truth with the sole purpose of glorifying God.

Compassionate confrontation is not for the few but for everyone who names the name of Christ as their Savior. We are called to be salt and light. (Matthew 5) Light exposes the evil deeds of darkness and sheds light on the reality of a sinner's predicament. (Ephesians 5:11) Salt heals and preserves. Without the confrontation of light and salt, those who grope in darkness are left without hope.

A Call for Radicals

Being called a radical is not a bad thing. It means that you are springing forth from the Root. While we abide in the Vine, we stand as a lighthouse to those who have drifted far away from the harbor of righteousness. I agree with the call for a generation of radicals who will compassionately confront a dying world with the life-giving Truth of God's Word.

We need a revolutionary message in the world of relativity; a hot message in the lukewarm culture of today. We profess to believe in God and then go about our lives as though He does not exist. Our churches are so organized according to the business practices of the world that it would appear that everything that happens can be duplicated on Madison Avenue. Opportunities for ministry wait in line to find the right champion in the inner circle and then are evaluated based upon how they might impact or benefit the church and whether they fit into the budget.

In my thirty years of ministry, it is rare to find church leadership that prays over ministry opportunities and gets involved because God moved them, even though it may stretch the budget and is a risky venture. If everything that happens can be calculated, then there is no room for God to glorify Himself.

God's call is to walk on water with Him, to go to a land that He will reveal on the way there, to spend nights with lions, to stand in the midst of fiery furnaces, to be stoned to death and yet live to preach about it, to be a witness in high school that God can use around the world, to lose our life so that we can find it.

We need a revolutionary message that does more than teach the doctrines of Scripture but applies them to the hard, hard issues of life. When the Scriptures say that divorce is wrong, then we must not practice divorce in the church, but be ready to wrestle with the difficult issues that face couples in trouble.

When the Scriptures say abortion is murder, we must act as though it is murder, and be ready to assist girls and couples who are faced with the challenge of an unexpected child. When the Scriptures say the practice of homosexuality is wrong, we must condemn it as such, and be ready to reach out to those who are held in bondage by the sin, and give them a way out.

When the Scriptures teach us to love our enemies, we must be willing to suffer without revenge. We must give the world a message that has feet, a message that people can see before they hear. We must show an apathetic world the radical message of God's righteousness and love by the way we live.

Are radicals loud, bold and outgoing? Not always. Radicals, like people, come in all shapes and sizes, all ages, and all personality types. What makes them radical is their confidence in God's Word and His work. They are not desperately trying to win battles and manipulate life. They are confidently engaged in being what God desires them to be in the midst of the circumstances He has brought their way. As we come to the end of this book, it is time to do some evaluation and introspection.

How confident are you in the truthfulness of God's Word in all areas of life? How are you handling the circumstances in which you find yourself? Did God create the earth? Is homosexuality a sinful chosen behavior? Is divorce wrong? Is living together a sin? Is abortion murder? Is God in control? How much do you accommodate the world's values in these areas and disregard what the Bible says? Radicals do not have to be loud, but they do have to have radical confidence in God and His Word.

Radicals live innocent lives before God and toward man. Are there things in your life that are hidden from others because you know they are wrong? They may be hidden from others, but they are not hidden from God. Are you innocent before men? What is your relationship with your boss, your spouse, your parents, your neighbor, your Christian friends, the people who mock or hate you, those who have harmed you, or your ex-spouse? Are you at odds with anyone in your church? Radicals do not have to be bold, but they do have a radically innocent life before God and toward man.

Radicals are compassionate. Radicals see people as God sees them. When was the last time you helped a stranger, talked to a homeless person, became concerned enough about a neighbor to visit, spoke to a homosexual about how life is treating them, or spent time with an older person or a younger person? Radicals do not have to be dynamic, but they do have to have a radical compassion for people.

Radicals bring glory to God. Radicals realize that God is glorified in their lives when they acknowledge Him in all things, show His Love to all people, and honor Him with their lives. How often do you ask yourself, "How can God be glorified in this situation, relationship, problem, or sickness? Radicals do not have to be aggressive, but they do have to have a radical desire to see God glorified.

There is not a program or technology that can bring power to God's church. Nor is there a style of music or a style of worship that will bring spiritual life to God's people. We must stop accommodating the world and begin obeying God's Word, while we put aside the unbiblical divisiveness that causes brothers and sisters in Christ to live in contention over non-essential issues.

Our times cry for a core of people, led by the Spirit of God, who will compassionately confront error with Truth, and are willing to be persecuted by both the religious and secular worlds. God is still searching for someone who will stand in the gap at such a time as this. (Ezekiel 22:23-30)

Jesus, our Redeemer, modeled the walk of the redeemed when he suffered the reproach of both the secular and religious worlds. Never did any man show more compassion to sinners and yet live an uncompromised life of godly integrity and character. The sinner saw Him as hope, the religious saw Him as a threat, and yet He became a Savior to both as they realized He was Truth. The writer of Hebrews reminds us that to follow His path will take us outside the gates.

Therefore Jesus also, that He might sanctify the people through His own blood, suffered outside the gate. Hence, let us go out to Him outside the camp, bearing His reproach. For here we do not have a lasting city, but we are seeking the city which is to come. Through Him then, let us continually offer up a sacrifice of praise to God, that is, the fruit of lips that give thanks to His name. Hebrews 13:12-16

Chuck Colson in his book, <u>How Now Shall We Live,</u> sums up our current need when he says, "If our culture is to be transformed, it will happen from the bottom up – from ordinary believers practicing apologetics over the backyard fence or barbeque grill."

Now to Him who is able to keep you from stumbling,
and to make you stand in the presence of His glory
blameless with great joy, to the only God our Savior,
through Jesus Christ our Lord,
be glory, majesty, dominion and authority,
before all time and now and forever. Amen.

Jude 24-25

Epilogue

—⟋⟍—

I am writing this epilogue to prevent any misunderstanding about what I have written. The casual reader may believe that I am condemning the church, advocating rebellious confrontation, or suggesting an impractical lifestyle in the twenty-first century.

The Church

There are those who are advocating that the church is no longer God's plan for our day. They believe that the organized church is no longer relevant and that people are finding their spiritual needs met outside the church. I view this as a restlessness in the true church. There is a change coming within the church. God is at work preparing His bride. Remember what God said about the Bride of His Son:

> Husbands, love your wives, just as Christ also loved the church and gave Himself up for her; that He might sanctify her, having cleansed her by the washing of water with the word, <u>that He might present to Himself the church in all her glory, having no spot or wrinkle or any such thing;</u> but that she should be holy and blameless. Ephesians 5:25-28 *emphasis mine*

There is no biblical basis to believe that God is done with the church, but there is biblical basis to believe that the church can expect God to shake it up in these last days. Matthew 13:31-32 says the kingdom of heaven is like a mustard seed which grows into a very large tree in which the birds come to roost. The church has grown far beyond the small seed that was planted over two thousand years ago.

Emperor Constantine knew he had to deal with the church's presence in Rome, and in 313 AD he made Christianity a legal religion. This caused it to flourish and become so politically polluted that by the time of the reformation, it no longer contained the essence of the Seed and had perverted the Gospel. Today, the birds still find a social resting place, a place of status and belonging, and a religious balm for their guilty souls within the established church. In many churches, they control the vote, control the pastor, and cool the message. They are the cause for the lukewarm condition that sickens God. (Revelation 3:16) It is no wonder the watching world says that church is for the birds.

God is not done with the church, but He is preparing it for the great wedding that has been planned since eternity past. As He begins to shake the tree of His Kingdom, the birds will fly out. We have been told of a time like this in the Scriptures:

> Do not love the world, nor the things in the world. If anyone loves the world, the love of the Father is not in him. For all that is in the world, the lust of the flesh and the lust of the eyes and the boastful pride of life, is not from the Father, but is from the world. And the world is passing away, and also its lusts; but the one who does the will of God abides forever.
> Children, it is the last hour; and just as you heard that antichrist is coming, even now many antichrists have arisen; from this we know that it is the last hour. <u>They</u>

went out from us, but they were not really of us; for
if they had been of us, they would have remained
with us; but they went out, in order that it might be
shown that they all are not of us. But you have an
anointing from the Holy One, and you all know. I
have not written to you because you do not know the
truth, but because you do know it, and because no lie
is of the truth. 1 John 2:15-21 *(emphasis mine)*

There will be a shaking up of the visible church. In some
cases the birds will win, and an organized religious society
will occupy the building that once housed the church. We
have already seen these phenomena as liberalism and religious societies, totally void of the Gospel or Truth, occupy
edifices with steeples and stained glass. At other times, the
Truth will stand, and those who are not of the Truth will
leave. Again, this is nothing new. Even Jesus offended some
when He taught Truth. The following is an account of people
leaving because the Truth was too hard:

These things He said in the synagogue, as He
taught in Capernaum. Many therefore of His disciples, when they heard this said, "This is a difficult
statement; who can listen to it?" But Jesus, conscious
that His disciples grumbled at this, said to them,
"Does this cause you to stumble? What then if you
should behold the Son of Man ascending where He
was before? It is the Spirit who gives life; the flesh
profits nothing; the words that I have spoken to you
are spirit and are life. But there are some of you who
do not believe." For Jesus knew from the beginning
who they were who did not believe, and who it was
that would betray Him. And He was saying, "For this
reason I have said to you, that no one can come to
Me, unless it has been granted him from the Father."

As a result of this many of His disciples withdrew, and were not walking with Him anymore. Jesus said therefore to the twelve, "You do not want to go away also, do you?" Simon Peter answered Him, "Lord, to whom shall we go? You have words of eternal life. "And we have believed and have come to know that You are the Holy One of God." John 6:59-70 *emphasis mine.*

In both cases, it is God at work in His church. God is applying a spot remover which exposes the sins that are spots on his Bride, and He is applying the hot iron of persecution to remove the wrinkles of an unkempt church. The church has not been abandoned by God. It will face some significant challenges in the near future, but the challenges are intended to make it better not worse. The Scriptures do not speak of a comfortable lifestyle for the Christian as the end draws near. Consider the admonition found in 1 Peter:

Beloved, do not be surprised at the fiery ordeal among you, which comes upon you for your testing, as though some strange thing were happening to you; but to the degree that you share the sufferings of Christ, keep on rejoicing; so that also at the revelation of His glory, you may rejoice with exultation. If you are reviled for the name of Christ, you are blessed, because the Spirit of glory and of God rests upon you. By no means let any of you suffer as a murderer, or thief, or evildoer, or a troublesome meddler; but if anyone suffers as a Christian, let him not feel ashamed, but in that name let him glorify God. For it is time for judgment to begin with the household of God; and if it begins with us first, what will be the outcome for those who do not obey the gospel of God? And if it is with difficulty that the righteous is saved, what will become of the godless man and the sinner? Therefore, let those also who suffer according to the will of God entrust their souls to a faithful Creator in doing what is right. 1 Peter 4:12-19

These are exciting days for the church of the Lord Jesus Christ. Some have said they would like to have lived in the first century church. I believe the saints of the first century would give anything to live in the twenty-first century church. These are the days they envisioned and for which they waited earnestly. These are the days just prior to Christ's second coming.

Rebellious Confrontation

Because I was involved in Operation Rescue and was an anti-abortion leader, some will wonder if I condone abortion clinic bombings or shooting of abortionists. This is because the media presented non-violent Christian people as violent and then lumped them together with people who bombed abortion clinics and murdered abortionists.

We are not called to bomb buildings or shoot people. The pro-life movement of the late 1980's was very unusual. It brought together diverse segments of the Christian community and created dialog that was spiritually enriching. It began with the premise, "If abortion is murder why don't we act like it is murder?" It was based on the command of Proverbs 24:11,12 which says:

Deliver those who are being taken away to death,
And those who are staggering to slaughter,
O hold them back.
If you say, "See, we did not know this,"
Does He not consider it who weighs the hearts?
And does He not know it who keeps your soul?

And will He not render to man according to his
work?

Intervening on the behalf of helpless unborn children
and their misled mothers is an act of love and obedience. As
the police liaison for the movement, I was at the core of the
issues concerning how far we could go to protect children's
lives as Christian people. Respect for authority and Christian
integrity are what God uses to win battles.

The movement attracted some militant personalities, but
while I was associated with it, there was a non-violent pact
that was mandatory for anyone to sign if they planned on
participating. The stories in the media and the rumors that
spread through the churches are far from factual.

Practical Applications

Finally, there is the issue of the practical application of
these principles. It would appear, at first glance, that we are
unable to live with confidence concerning things the world
says it has proven to be wrong. It seems as though, if we fail
to retaliate against our enemies, they will win. Some would
say of this book, "It sounds good, but it is impractical in the
real world."

There are two phrases that really bother me in the church
today. One is: "I live in the real world." As though what the
Scriptures say only works in a fantasy world or in the church
world. The other is the word "but," which comes at the end
of a spiritual truth and just before the reason why the spiritual truth will not work in this particular case. I am in the
process of researching this topic in a study I am calling, "No
buts about it."

The leaders of the Israelites professed to believe as David
did when he said God could slay the giant, BUT they were
not willing to act on that belief. The three Hebrew children
were not intimidated by the circumstances of the furnace.

They knew God could deliver them, no buts about it. God's principles are practical, and God intends for us to apply them to our lives.

It is not always easy, but it is always rewarding to obey God and watch Him work. I wear out the insides of my shoes from curling up my toes as I attempt to apply God's Word to various situations. <u>Confidence</u> takes away the necessity for extreme emotion. <u>Innocence</u> takes away the defensive attitude. <u>Compassion</u> does away with selfish motives, and <u>focusing</u> on God's glory puts it all in perspective.

Start practicing these four guiding principles at home and around friends. As your confidence in God grows, apply them to your relationships with your neighbors and co-workers. As these principles become a part of your life-style, you will see the Lord use you to bring glory to Himself and to minister to people you would have normally avoided, even your enemies.

Referenced Sources

—ɯ—

American Civil Liberties Union. (2005, March 2). In *ACLU's defense of religious liberty*. Retrieved January 16, 2005, from American Civil Liberties Union Web Site: http://www.aclu.com/religion/tencomm/16254res20050302.html

Colson, C. (1999). *How now shall we live*. Wheaton, Ill: Tyndell House Publishers.

Barna, G. (2005). *Revolution*. Wheaton, Ill: Tyndell House Publishers.

Butterfield, L. H. (Ed.). (1963). *Adams family correspondence* (Vol I ed.). Cambridge: Harvard University Press.

Gannon, J. P. (2006, January 9). Is God dead in Europe? (What might that mean for America?). *USA Today,* p. A11.

Guinness, O. (2003). *Prophetic untimeliness: a challenge to the idol of relevance*. Grand Rapids: Baker Books.

Hocking, D. (1990). *The moral catastrophe*. Eugene, Oregon: Harvest House Publishers.

Hoyle, F. (1983). *The intelligent universe*. New York: Holt, Rinehart and Winston.

Macarthur, J. (2000). *Why government can't save you*. Nashville: Word Publishing.

New American standard bible - updated edition. (1999). Grand Rapids: Zondervan Publishing House.

Nicholi, Armand (September 2004). *The question of God.* Public Broadcasting Station, WGBH Educational Foundation.

The Voice Of The Martyrs (2003). *Forever young: Living and dying for Christ.* Gainesville, Florida: Bridge-Logos Publishing.

Whitehead, J. W. (1982). *Second American revolution.* Elgin, Illinois: David C. Cook Publishing Co.

Dawson, S. C. (1988). *God's providence in America's history.* Rancho Cordova, CA: Steve C. Dawson.

Price, R. (Ed.). (1793). *Works of the late Doctor Benjamin Franklin consisting of his life, written by himself, together with essays, humorous, moral and literary, chiefly in the manner of the spectator.* Dublin: P.Wogan, P. Byme, J. Moore and W. Jones.

Schenck, P., & Schenck, R. (1993). *The extermination of christianity.* Lafeyette, Louisiana: Hunington House Publishers.

—ɯ—

Jim Evans is available for speaking engagements including:
church meetings, conference speaking, workshops,
debates, or consulting.
He can be reached via e-mail at:

questions4jim@yahoo.com

Printed in the United States
87893LV00002B/166-249/A